MARCH 2018

Contested Seas

Maritime Domain Awareness in Northern Europe

PROJECT DIRECTOR
Kathleen H. Hicks

AUTHORS
Andrew Metrick
Kathleen H. Hicks

A Report of the
CSIS INTERNATIONAL SECURITY PROGRAM

CSIS | CENTER FOR STRATEGIC &
INTERNATIONAL STUDIES

ROWMAN &
LITTLEFIELD

Lanham • Boulder • New York • London

About CSIS

For over 50 years, the Center for Strategic and International Studies (CSIS) has worked to develop solutions to the world's greatest policy challenges. Today, CSIS scholars are providing strategic insights and bipartisan policy solutions to help decisionmakers chart a course toward a better world.

CSIS is a nonprofit organization headquartered in Washington, D.C. The Center's 220 fulltime staff and large network of affiliated scholars conduct research and analysis and develop policy initiatives that look into the future and anticipate change.

Founded at the height of the Cold War by David M. Abshire and Admiral Arleigh Burke, CSIS was dedicated to finding ways to sustain American prominence and prosperity as a force for good in the world. Since 1962, CSIS has become one of the world's preeminent international institutions focused on defense and security; regional stability; and transnational challenges ranging from energy and climate to global health and economic integration.

Thomas J. Pritzker was named chairman of the CSIS Board of Trustees in November 2015. Former U.S. deputy secretary of defense John J. Hamre has served as the Center's president and chief executive officer since 2000.

CSIS does not take specific policy positions. Accordingly, all views, positions, and conclusions expressed in this publication should be understood to be solely those of the author(s).

ISBN: 978-1-4422-8067-0 (pb); 978-1-4422-8068-7 (eBook)

Center for Strategic & International Studies
1616 Rhode Island Avenue, NW
Washington, DC 20036
202-887-0200 | www.csis.org

Rowman & Littlefield
4501 Forbes Boulevard
Lanham, MD 20706
301-459-3366 | www.rowman.com

Contents

Executive Summary

Northern Europe, and specifically the Baltic and Norwegian Seas, has been the site of increasingly provocative and destabilizing Russian actions. The country's use of a range of military, diplomatic, and economic tools to undermine the North Atlantic Treaty Organization (NATO) and its allies highlights the need to monitor and understand Russian activity. The region is characterized by complex factors like unique geographic features, considerable civilian maritime traffic, the presence of advanced Russian and Western military capabilities, and strategic proximity to Russia and the Kola peninsula, home to the Russian Northern Fleet. While the Norwegian and Baltic Seas do differ in key ways, they are linked by the emerging risk posed by Russia's long-range strike capabilities.

Responding to Russian challenges across the competitive space requires a deep understanding of the Northern European maritime environment. Maritime Domain Awareness (MDA), defined by the United States as the effective understanding of anything associated with the maritime domain that could impact the security, safety, economy, or environment of a nation or region, is an exceptionally broad concept. At its core, MDA has three functions: the collection of raw data, the analysis of that data, and the action of disseminating information to and coordinating among the different components of the framework. In order to provide security in Northern Europe, NATO and its allies must use MDA frameworks to understand and respond to the challenges above, on, and underneath the sea, as well as the surrounding land environment. While some constructive work has been done to address the evolving Russian threat, NATO and its partners must make changes to their current MDA capabilities to evolve alongside with it.

Russia presents three challenges of particular concern to the MDA efforts in Northern Europe: maritime hybrid warfare, electronic and cyber warfare capabilities, and long-range strike systems.

1. Maritime Hybrid Warfare—The Russian military is experienced and effective in its use of hybrid warfare, seen in Syria, Crimea, and Northern Europe. The ambiguity possible in the maritime domain lends itself well to this strategy. Russia uses three specific approaches in this realm: deception through different types of vessels including civilian ships, deniable forces like the amphibious and light infantry that easily navigate the complex Baltic and Norwegian Seas, and the country's well-developed and diverse force for seabed warfare.

2. Cyber and Electronic Warfare—Russia's advanced EW capabilities have the potential to hinder information gathering and dissemination methods, which are both vital functions of MDA. These capabilities are challenging for military personnel but potentially devastating in civilian contexts, especially as civilian networks and technology (like GPS) are far less secure.

3. Long-Range Strike Capabilities—New challenges for NATO and Northern European partners have emerged with Russia's development of a long-range precision strike complex. The weapons, now being mounted on new and existing Russian naval vessels, give these vessels the option to stay in the Barents or White Seas and strike targets across Northern Europe.

This, combined with air force capabilities based on the Kola Peninsula and in Kaliningrad, presents threats unlike any seen by NATO before. These capabilities require NATO and its partners to use MDA frameworks to monitor launch platforms across the domain.

The modern history of MDA begins in the United States, with Homeland Security Presidential Directive – 13 (HSPD-13) / National Security Presidential Directive – 41 (NSPD-41) issued in 2004 by President George W. Bush. The document lays out core interests for the United States to enhance security in the maritime domain and creates a cooperative framework to support MDA operations across different spheres. At the same time, the European concept of maritime security awareness was built upon the U.S. definition of the challenge, placed within the context of rising illicit traffic in the Mediterranean.

A weakness of the original MDA and Maritime Situational Awareness (MSA) concepts is that many of the associated capabilities and frameworks are focused on civil maritime issues. Given the global proliferation of advanced military capabilities, like antiship cruise missiles, NATO and its partners require a holistic understanding of the maritime environment that focuses on everything from civil maritime actions to high-end military operations and even issues *associated* with the maritime environment.

A key implication of the heightened maritime threat environment is the need to improve the integration of and attention to undersea aspects of MDA. Antisubmarine warfare (ASW), a traditional strength of Western naval intelligence and operations, has atrophied since the end of the Cold War. Today, Russian submarines with conventional long-range missiles pose a threat to NATO. ASW must be integrated with MDA to address these concerns. Comprehensive understanding of the undersea realm should extend beyond ASW. Russia's amphibious special forces and combat swimmers threaten more than just military targets, including civilian vessels and undersea cables, which are an integral part of MDA. ASW technology can be useful in countering these and other threats.

In the Norwegian Sea, the biggest challenge for NATO is detecting advanced ultra-quiet submarines. This issue is sharpened by dramatically depleted stockpiles of sonobuoys, a constant need for increasingly advanced sonobuoy technology, and an American unwillingness to share highly classified information about the undersea domain. NATO would benefit from an apparatus like the ASW Operations Centers (ASWOC), used most prominently during the Cold War to streamline ASW operations. Integration of platforms is a challenge in the Baltic Sea as well, largely because Sweden and Finland are not NATO states, making data sharing challenging. Frameworks like Sea Surveillance Co-Operation Baltic Sea (SUCBAS) and the Maritime Surveillance (MARSUR) project facilitate the work of regional states to address these issues but more must be done. Additionally, NATO monitoring of the Baltic region is largely domain specific and suffers from not examining the maritime domain holistically. The alliance and its partners should also act to focus on resiliency to continue to operate in the face of jamming and nonkinetic attacks from Russia.

The key to enhancing MDA capabilities in Northern Europe is the integration of frameworks across the maritime domain. Cooperation between NATO states and allies is vital to understanding the complex environment. The CSIS study team has identified seven recommendations of particular importance:

- Create a Baltic Sea MDA analytic center at the Baltic Maritime Component Command (BMCC) at Rostock, Germany;

- Empower a small analytic team at the BMCC to focus on maritime hybrid issues;

- Develop a training course for military intelligence officers on best practices for Baltic Sea MDA analysis;

- Create a classified Baltic Sea data environment that can incorporate both NATO and partner states;

- Develop a multinational operational framework for the Baltic Sea;

- Integrate subsurface sensors and antisubmarine warfare into a comprehensive MDA framework; and

- Acquire significant stockpiles of advanced sonobuoys and associated acoustic processing systems.

These priority recommendations are presented in detail in Chapter 4 of the report, along with others. Collectively, their implication would markedly enhance security in Northern Europe by closing identified gaps and ensuring capabilities for collection, analysis, and action in MDA.

Acknowledgments

The authors would like to thank numerous experts in Finland, Germany, Italy, Poland, Sweden, the United Kingdom, and the United States for sharing their time and insights at various points throughout the study. In particular, the CSIS team thanks the Centre for Maritime Research and Experimentation (CMRE), U.S. Naval Forces Europe (NAVUER), and the Polish government for helping facilitate a series of productive meetings in Italy and Poland. This study has been dramatically improved by insights shared in a host of interviews and workshops.

The project would not have been possible without the excellent leadership of Lisa Sawyer Samp, formerly a senior fellow in the International Security Program at CSIS. Ms. Samp led the project team from July 2017 until her departure in November 2017. The team is also deeply grateful to Anthony Bell, Andrew Linder, Eric Jacobson, and Sarah Atac for their editorial and research support. Mr. Bell also facilitated and participated in the study team's engagements in Europe.

Finally, the study team wishes to acknowledge Saab, the study's sponsor, which saw the value in growing a more detailed knowledge of maritime issues in Northern Europe. The team is deeply appreciative of Saab's respect for our intellectual independence at each step along the way. The content and recommendations presented—including any errors—remain solely those of the authors.

Introduction

Since Russia's illegal annexation of Crimea in 2014, the transatlantic security community has been increasingly concerned with Russia's malign influence and actions across the region. Russia's use of a broad range of military, diplomatic, economic, and informational tools to undermine the NATO alliance and its European partners has been observed from Southern Europe and the Balkans to Northern Europe and the Arctic. Protecting trade flows, military freedom of maneuver, and critical infrastructure in the Baltic and Norwegian Seas are particular areas of concern. Russia's deployment of a wide array of new and upgraded capabilities above, on, and under the waves creates challenges for the United States and European nations in these maritime regions. In addition, these abilities are buttressed by land-based systems that can project power across the littorals.

The Baltic Sea is one of the world's most challenging maritime operational environments, due to such factors as its high salinity, shallowness, and array of unexploded twentieth-century ordinance. It is the architype of a contested littoral environment. A vital trade route with considerable undersea infrastructure, the sheer scale of Baltic maritime traffic makes identifying, tracking, and understanding potentially hostile activities difficult. The energy flows through this basin are the third densest in the world, behind the Strait of Hormuz and Strait of Malacca.[1] The Baltic Sea also lies along a seam in the transatlantic security architecture, abutted by both NATO nations and NATO's partners, Sweden and Finland.

The Norwegian Sea derives strategic importance from its location relative to the Kola Peninsula, home to Russia's Northern Fleet, the preponderance of its naval forces. NATO and its partners rely on access to the North Atlantic, including the Norwegian Sea, to flow forces and support to the continent in the event of any sizable military contingency. Russia, in turn, has an incentive to ensure its ability to sail the Northern Fleet through the Norwegian Sea and into the Atlantic. The Norwegian Sea is a much different environment than the Baltic. However, these two problems are intrinsically linked because of the evolving nature of Russia's long-range strike capabilities. These systems, capable of being launched from ground, aerial, and naval platforms, expand the littoral battlespace. They necessitate NATO and regional partners to integrate a range of capabilities in new ways.

As Russia adapts its strategy and capabilities—from use of hybrid tactics to growing long-range strike capabilities and inventory—the nature of the challenges facing NATO and its European partners in these maritime theaters merits review. That review should begin with assessing the foundation on which Western maritime capability will rest: effective maritime domain awareness (MDA). The U.S. Navy defines MDA as the effective understanding of anything associated with the maritime domain that could impact the security, safety, economy, or environment of a nation or

---

[1] Lejla Villar and Marson Hamilton, "The Danish and Turkish Straits are critical to Europe's crude oil and petroleum trade," U.S. Energy Information Administration, August 18, 2017, https://www.eia.gov/todayinenergy/detail.php?id=32552.

region.[2] This study uses the term *MDA networks* to capture the range of users, platforms, and sensors that are required to achieve effective MDA. The term does not refer to a specific data-sharing environment or a discrete network arrangement. MDA networks in Northern Europe need to navigate multiple national, bilateral, and regional security arrangements, including law enforcement and military functions. Establishing a cohesive single network is almost certainly not the best near-term goal for MDA networking in Northern Europe.

To chart a path ahead, the International Security Program at the Center for Strategic and International Studies undertook at nine-month study that included open-source research, numerous interviews with experts in the United States and across Europe, a week-long study trip that included stops at the Centre for Maritime Research and Experimentation (CMRE), U.S. Navy Europe (NAVEUR), and Warsaw. The effort built on prior analysis conducted by the study team, including in support of the 2016 CSIS report *Undersea Warfare in Northern Europe*.[3] The team is deeply indebted to all of those who contributed their insight and expertise for this study. While benefiting from this tremendous wealth of knowledge, the opinions, findings, and recommendations of this study are solely those of the authors.

Throughout the study process, three interrelated questions served as guideposts. First, what are the specific operational, technological, capability, logistics, infrastructure, and policy requirements for creating an MDA network in a contested littoral environment? Second, how does geography and threat shape the requirements for these networks in two different basins, the Baltic Sea and Norwegian Sea? Third, are there common elements that can be applied across different regions and what is the implication of this commonality for NATO and NATO partner approaches?

To help elucidate the challenge set, the CSIS study team divided MDA into three functions: *collection*, *analysis*, and *action*. These terms are defined as follows:

> *Collection* refers to gathering raw data on the maritime domain to include subsurface, surface, and aerial targets of interest. Traditionally, collection has been approached from a platform-centric perspective. Platforms are important as their characteristics affect the capabilities of hosted payloads. However, a payload-centric view of collection is more appropriate as payload modularity increases and platforms are expected to respond across the range of military operations. This analytic approach focuses on the sensors required to meet MDA requirements before turning to platforms themselves. The key question for determining the adequacy of collection capabilities is whether the sensor architecture provides the coverage and responsiveness necessary to meet the threats.

> *Analysis* refers to the ability to take the raw data gathered by collection assets, create a common picture, and derive greater insights into the state of the maritime domain. This is the difference between raw data and actionable intelligence. The team understands analysis to include both computer-driven automated processing capabilities and human-driven intelligence fusion centers. At the macro level, analysis is the process by which localized

---

[2] U.S. Department of the Navy, *Navy Maritime Domain Awareness Concept* (Washington, DC: May 2017), http://www.navy.mil/navydata/cno/Navy_Maritime_Domain_Awareness_Concept_FINAL_2007.pdf.
[3] Kathleen H. Hicks et al, *Undersea Warfare in Northern Europe* (Washington, DC: Center for Strategic and International Studies, July 2016), https://www.csis.org/analysis/undersea-warfare-northern-europe.

awareness of the environment becomes operational and strategic understanding. The key question for determining the adequacy of analysis capabilities is whether the analytic architecture can incorporate a wide range of sensor inputs in a timely fashion to produce actionable intelligence.

Action refers to the ability to take the products developed by the analytic team, disseminate them to the relevant places and platforms, and if necessary, take appropriate steps to mitigate an identified threat. It also covers the legal and policy frameworks necessary to take effective action in the context of universally recognized rules and norms. The primary components of action are the datalinks that knit together the broad components of the MDA network, the partnership agreements that bring together different national capabilities, and the unified, multinational political will to confront identified challenges. Awareness for the sake of awareness will not help address pressing operational challenges in the Baltic Sea and North Atlantic. The key questions for determining the adequacy of action are whether the network infrastructure supports adequate dissemination in both peacetime and wartime, and whether there effective political, legal, and operational frameworks in place.

To understand the need for an enhanced MDA capability in the Baltic Sea and North Atlantic, Chapter 1 lays out the Russian military capabilities largely driving these upgrades and enhancements. Chapter 2 explores the history of MDA and the requirements for MDA in these basins. Chapter 3 discusses the existing capabilities and agreements in relevant nations across Northern Europe. Finally, Chapter 4 offers recommendations for improving and optimizing these capabilities to better meet the evolving threat and to close known gaps in the existing MDA architecture.

Chapter 1: The Russia Challenge

Russia is the primary challenge driving a reexamination of maritime domain awareness capabilities throughout the Baltic and Norwegian Sea regions. As demonstrated by Russia's provocative and destabilizing actions, there is a need to monitor and understand Russian activity. Because of the Northern Fleet's disproportionate importance to the Russian Navy and Baltic Sea's seam, MDA in these regions is vital. The Baltic Sea region is particularly stressing due to the congruence of factors involved, ranging from considerable civil ship traffic to the presence of advanced military capabilities. The complex nature of this region makes it potentially susceptible to Russian hybrid tactics that seek to achieve objectives with a modicum of risk. MDA is vital to countering such approaches as they can only be effectively countered if political leadership feels that they have a solid understand of Russian activities and intent.

Russia retains a broad range of strategic, conventional, and irregular capabilities to challenge the political resolve of NATO and its regional partners. This study does not seek to present a comprehensive assessment of Russian capabilities.[4] Instead, this chapter delineates three areas of concern particularly relevant to the maritime domain awareness challenge in Northern Europe: maritime hybrid warfare, electronic and cyber warfare capabilities, and long-range strike systems.

It is vital to approach the Russia challenge set in a measured and careful manner. As stressed in *Undersea Warfare in Northern Europe*, many Russian activities that Western actors view as destabilizing or provocative could be explained as a return to acceptable readiness and improved standard operating procedures dormant after the Cold War but reasonable for a nation interested in self-defense. The increased operational tempo of Russian submarines and its use of these vessels to monitor NATO naval activities in international waters, for example, might be explained in this way. Indeed, some Russian actions that have concerned NATO and its partners are comparable to actions they themselves have undertaken. For example, the U.S. Air Force routinely operates intelligence aircraft close to Russia while remaining in international, allied, or partner airspace.

However, one must not downplay Russian actions that go beyond the normal boundaries of peacetime military preparedness. In fact, Russia often operates a given platform within the bounds of international rules and norms on one day only to operate that same platform in a destabilizing and provocative manner the next day. This underscores the need for effective MDA to understand and respond to Russian actions in a calibrated and appropriate manner. For example, Russian military aircraft are free to operate in international airspace to conduct a variety of training and strategic signaling missions.[5] However, Russian military aircraft should not be free to conduct mock nuclear attack runs on Danish territory during a major political festival.[6] The context-

---

[4] Such an assessment is provided in several previous reports from the study team, including Lisa Sawyer Samp and Beverly Kirk, "Recalibrating U.S. Strategy toward Russia and Undersea Warfare in Northern Europe," https://www.csis.org/podcasts/smart-women-smart-power-podcast/recalibrating-us-strategy-toward-russia.

[5] 1.2.1 Civil/Military Cooperation in Air Traffic Management (International Civil Aviation Organization 2011), https://www.icao.int/apac/meetings/2012_cmc/cir330_en.pdf.

[6] "Russia simulated an attack on Denmark," *The Local Denmark*, October 31, 2014, https://www.thelocal.dk/20141031/russia-simulated-a-military-attack-on-denmark.

dependent nature of Russian military actions will put a premium on tailoring responses to avoid unnecessary and/or unintended escalation.

In the following analytic sections, this study explores how Russian maritime hybrid warfare, cyber and electronic warfare, and long-range strike capabilities each poses a unique challenge for the existing MDA network in these regions. Furthermore, these sections consider how Russia may employ these capabilities on a range of novel platforms that will further stress the ability of NATO and partners to perceive the maritime domain. While these capabilities are presented individually, it is important to acknowledge that the synthesis of discrete capabilities creates pernicious challenges for NATO and its partners. The twenty-first-century Russian way of war is not predicated solely on exquisite capabilities. Rather, Russia leverages a combination of old and new capabilities to maximize strategic uncertainty, create localized surprise, and ultimately achieve targeted tactical overmatch. This combination of uncertainty, surprise, and overmatch severely stresses an adversary's awareness and decisionmaking process.

Maritime Hybrid Warfare

The maritime domain lends itself well to a variety of hybrid tactics. For the purposes of this study, hybrid warfare is understood to be a range of military and nonmilitary actions that fall in the miasma between clear war and certain peace.[7] The inherent uncertainty of the maritime domain lends itself well to the application of hybrid tactics. Given the large number of vessels operating at sea, it can be easy to hide in plain sight. Furthermore, it may be possible to camouflage military capabilities about erstwhile civilian vessels. These attempts at obfuscation dramatically curtail the political decision space and may severely challenge crisis response. Hybrid operational approaches in the maritime domain include more "traditional" irregular maritime warfare capabilities such as mine warfare, amphibious SOF, and combat swimmers. Russia has demonstrated a proficiency with land-centric hybrid warfare capabilities in operations in Crimea and, to a lesser degree, Eastern Ukraine. This section considers three potential Russian approaches to maritime hybrid warfare: deception, deniable forces, and seabed warfare.

Deception is as old as warfare itself. In the maritime domain, there are numerous ways of hiding in plain sight. One of the most troubling is the containerization of advanced missile systems. Russia has recently showcased several containerized missile systems that outwardly appear indistinguishable from a normal shipping container.[8] A number of these containers could be seeded throughout the Baltic Sea region at both port facilities and on Russian-operated vessels. Locating and tracking these specific containers would be incredibly difficult. This deceptive capability would enable Russian leadership to mass considerable combat power in the region without raising alarm. In a crisis scenario, the revelation of such capabilities in politically sensitive areas would create new military facts on the ground.

Russia could also use ostensibly nonmilitary, Russian state-owned vessels for a range of military missions. In 2017, the Finnish government rejected a visit request from a Russian sail training ship

---

[7] For more see Martin Murphy, Frank G. Hoffman, and Gary Schaub Jr., *Hybrid Maritime Warfare and the Baltic Sea Region* (Copenhagen, Denmark: Centre for Military Studies, November 2016), http://cms.polsci.ku.dk/publikationer /hybrid-maritim-krigsfoerelse/Hybrid_Maritime_Warfare_and_the_Baltic_Sea_Region.pdf.
[8] "Club-K, Naval Systems," Rosoboronexport, http://roe.ru/eng/catalog/naval-systems/shipborne-weapons/klab-k/.

to Mariehamn, a port in the demilitarized province of Aland.[9] Some security experts interpreted this as an attempt by the Russian government to gauge Finnish reaction. Russian state-owned vessels could be used for a variety of intelligence tasks or to potentially insert small teams of special operations forces on sensitive islands in the Baltic Sea. These types of activities are difficult to track and analyze given the need to understand ship movements and behavior over long periods integrating sensor and intelligence data from multiple nations.

Deceptive capabilities are likely to be paired with deniable forces and traditional special operations forces. This could potentially include regular naval infantry forces in the most stressing contingency scenarios.[10] During the Cold War, the Soviet Union developed robust amphibious warfare capabilities. This included maritime special operations forces and combat swimmers. Soviet war plans included an amphibious assault against Denmark.[11] Some sources claim that the Soviet Union practiced insertion of covert forces into Sweden during this period; these claims remain exceptionally difficult to verify. Today, Russia maintains combat swimmers, naval spetsnaz, and naval infantry in the Baltic Sea region.

Amphibious special forces and light infantry forces are a particularly useful tool in the Baltic Sea region given its highly archipelagic nature. These forces provide a scalable capability that can be used for missions ranging from clandestine reconnaissance and targeted provocations to limited kinetic activities and full-blown island seizure. This breadth of capability drives a requirement for NATO and regional partners to develop solid insights into Russian amphibious special forces particularly Russian deployment patterns. Achieving this understanding is quite challenging as these forces often use small vessels that could hide in plain sight among the considerable civil maritime traffic in the region. Furthermore, Russia operates the "Raptor" patrol boat, which is visually similar to the Swedish CB90 patrol vessel. These deniable and low-visibility combat forces could be used to seize territory in the Baltic Sea with little to no warning. Such capabilities could create new military facts on the ground that would prove tremendously challenging to reverse absent considerable political will.

Russian combat swimmers are an overlooked capability with exceptional utility in a range of operations. These units are particularly concerning to Polish, Lithuanian, and Swedish forces due to their proximity to the Russian enclave of Kaliningrad. Combat swimmers may carry out a range of kinetic activities aimed at crippling both military and civil port operations. These forces could also be used for clandestine intelligence activities such as placing and retrieving seabed acoustic sensors. In many ways, combat swimmers are the oldest and arguably most effective force for maritime hybrid operations. They played a major role in naval operations during the Second World War. For example, the Italian Navy used combat swimmers to great effect during World War II disabling two British battleships at anchor in Alexandria harbor.[12] The United States used

---

[9] "Finnish military rejects request for Russian tall ship visit to Åland," *Yle Uutiset*, August 28, 2017, https://yle.fi/uutiset/osasto/news/finnish_military_rejects_request_for_russian_tall_ship_visit_to_aland/980122.

[10] It should be noted that Russian naval infantry represents some of the more combat-capable forces in the ground combat element of the Russian Armed Forces. They have been used considerably in combat operations in Crimea and Syria.

[11] Central Intelligence Agency, Directorate of Intelligence, *Warsaw Pact: Planning for Operations Against Denmark*, April 1989, https://www.cia.gov/library/readingroom/docs/1989-04-01.pdf.

[12] Vincent P. O'Hara and Enrico Cernuschi, "Frogmen Against a Fleet: The Italian Attack on Alexandria 18/19 December 1941," *Naval War College Review* 68, no. 3 (June 2015).

Underwater Demolition Teams, the predecessors of the modern SEALs, extensively during amphibious operations in the Pacific theater. These forces are very difficult to detect and potentially to defend against, a defining characteristic of maritime hybrid operations.

Lastly, Russia has the most developed force for seabed warfare in the world. Seabed warfare dates to at least World War II and covers a range of missions including: the placement of acoustic sensors, the placement of communications and power infrastructure to support UUV operations, tapping undersea cables, defending friendly undersea infrastructure, and surveying undersea wreckage for intelligence purposes. The Russian force is organized as a separate component of the Russian military under the auspices of the Directorate for Deep Sea Research (GUGI).[13] These platforms are primarily based out of Russia's Northern Sea Fleet at Olenya Guba near Murmansk. However, Russia has undertaken these operations in the Baltic Sea as well. Most notably, interfering with the completion of the SweLit undersea power cable in 2015. Russia also has an interest in defense seabed operations in this region given the importance of the NordStream pipeline to Russian energy exports. Russia has publicly talked about some of these capabilities in the context of Arctic seabed operations, primarily for resource extraction. Western defense analysts believe that several of these vessels, notably those with exceptionally deep diving capabilities, remotely operative or autonomous underwater vehicles, and manipulators, could be used to either tap or outright sever vital communications linkages either in the Baltic Sea or North Atlantic.[14] This would be akin to U.S. seabed operations targeting Soviet communication infrastructure undertaken during the Cold War.[15]

Taken together, these irregular capabilities provide Russia a hybrid toolkit useful across the range of military operations. From the perspective of NATO and partner nations, the primary challenge posed by these maritime hybrid tools is the potential for ambiguity and plausible deniability that surrounds their employment, which provides Russia with options to confuse, slow, and potentially cripple Western political decisionmaking. Effective MDA in Northern Europe would limit the opportunity for ambiguity, providing political and military leaders reliable information and understanding about Russian maritime hybrid warfare activities. NATO and partner nations will need to conduct these missions on a regular basis to understand not only Russian patterns of behavior but also to gain insight into Russian intent.

Cyber and Electronic Warfare

During operations in Crimea and Eastern Ukraine, Russia demonstrates a complex variety of nonkinetic capabilities spanning the information, electromagnetic, and cyberspace domains.[16] When integrated, these systems aim to slow an adversary's decisionmaking by increasing doubt and uncertainty. Nonkinetic operations can also degrade the efficacy of advanced military systems

---

[13] Foreign Military Studies Office, "Russian Media Discuss Role of Hydronauts," *OE Watch* 3, no. 1 (August 2013), http://fmso.leavenworth.army.mil/OEWatch/201308/Russia_09.html.

[14] H. I. Sutton, "Spy Subs—Project 10831 Losharik," *Covert Shores* (blog), September 22, 2016, http://www.hisutton.com/Spy%20Sub%20-%20Project%2010831%20Losharik.html

[15] Matt Blitz, "How Secret Underwater Wiretapping Helped End the Cold War," *Popular Mechanics*, March 30, 2017, http://www.popularmechanics.com/technology/security/a25857/operation-ivy-bells-underwater-wiretapping/.

[16] Kathleen H. Hicks et al., "Case Studies on Russia's Use of Force" and "Russian Instruments of Power," chap. 2–3, in *Recalibrating U.S. Strategy Toward Russia* (Washington, DC: Center for Strategic and International Studies, March 2017), https://www.csis.org/analysis/recalibrating-us-strategy-toward-russia.

that are highly network- and sensor-reliant. This section primarily focuses on Russian capabilities for electronic warfare (EW) but briefly considers the potential effects of Russian cyberspace operations on relevant military and civil activities in both the Baltic Sea and North Atlantic.

Russia maintains a wide array of EW systems ranging from large strategic systems with effects spanning hundreds of kilometers to smaller tactical systems designed to defend a small unit or single artillery piece. Broadly speaking, Russian EW systems can be broken out into two categories: electronic intelligence (ELINT) and electronic attack (EA). ELINT capabilities collect an adversary's electronic emissions providing "targets" that the EA systems can then prosecute. In addition, ELINT systems can also provide targeting information for other platforms to potentially include air defense systems. Of greatest concern to NATO and partner nations are the large strategic systems that Russia has repeatedly showcased at major arms shows and demonstrated in combat operations in Ukraine. The high-powered jamming complex, Krasukha, has particularly concerning capabilities as it can purportedly interfere with satellite and terrestrial datalinks, airborne radars, and satellite radar imaging systems.[17] Such systems are vital enabling capabilities for Western military forces. Russia has placed considerable emphasis on interfering with U.S. long-range strike capabilities by jamming networks, radar targeting systems, and crucially blocking GPS signals.

From the perspective of maritime domain awareness, these capabilities are highly concerning. Effective MDA requires both sensor coverage to gather information and reliable networks to disseminate raw data and final analytic products. EW capabilities can undermine both pillars. They can jam shipboard and aerial radars as well as a variety of vital communications systems. There are indications that some communication systems in the Baltic states were degraded by Russian EW capabilities during the 2017 iteration of the Zapad exercise.[18]

Russia may employ targeted EW capabilities on a steady-state basis both in the North Atlantic basin and in the Baltic Sea region to interfere with radar installations that Moscow views as exceptionally irritating. The joint Norwegian-U.S. radar installations on Vardo offer a perfect vantage point to monitor Russian missile tests conducted in the Barents Sea.[19] Even more problematic from a Russian perspective are the two AEGIS Ashore facilities in Eastern Europe. The plethora of targets coupled with considerable Russian investments in EW systems all but guarantees their employment in a contingency against NATO or its partners in either the Baltic Sea or Norwegian Sea region.

While Russian EW capabilities have concerning military implications, they create challenging and potentially lethal ramifications in several civilian contexts. For example, Russia may choose to employ EW systems to interfere with NATO communications systems during an exercise, such as BALTOPS. This jamming could severely impact civilian air and sea transportation throughout the region. A similar and potentially even more disruptive scenario would involve Russia jamming or spoofing GPS signals in the region. Exceptionally powerful broadband jamming capabilities, such as those operated by Russian strategic EW forces, would have incredibly deleterious effects on a

---

[17] Samuel Bendett, "America Is Getting Outclassed by Russian Electronic Warfare," *The National Interest*, September 19, 2017, http://nationalinterest.org/feature/america-getting-outclassed-by-russian-electronic-warfare-22380.
[18] Interviews with Baltic security experts.
[19] Thomas Nilsen, "U.S. Spends $50 Million on Vardø Radar Upgrade," *Barents Observer*, February 27, 2013, http://barentsobserver.com/en/security/2013/02/us-spends-50-million-vardo-radar-upgrade-27-02.

range of commercial activities that use similar portions of electromagnetic spectrum as military systems.

There are some reports that Russian counter-position, navigation, and timing (PNT) capabilities are currently impacting commercial ship traffic in the eastern Black Sea.[20] Given the density of ship and air traffic in the Baltic Sea region, such a loss or corruption of navigation data there would have profound effects. Moreover, the impact on civilian activities may only grow in the coming years as air traffic control systems become increasingly reliant upon GPS systems. In addition, cargo ships are increasingly automated and reliant on systems such as GPS and the Automated Identification System (AIS), a ubiquitous VHF radio system that is used to ensure the safe operation of commercial ship traffic. AIS is discussed further in Chapter 2. This automation will only grow in the coming year with proposals for fully autonomous shipping vessels plying routes in the Baltic Sea.[21] It is also conceivable that Russian nonkinetic capabilities could spoof AIS and aircraft transponder transmissions to serve as decoys to distract from other Russian activities. Such spoofing could further improve the deceptive nature of Russian maritime hybrid operations.

In addition to EW capabilities, Russia also maintains a considerable offensive cyberspace capability. This has been demonstrated in the Baltic Sea Region before, notably in the 2007 cyberattacks on Estonia.[22] While Russian offensive cyberspace capabilities have been most notably demonstrated against softer civilian targets, it is believed that Russia maintains a core of exquisite cyberspace capabilities that can target advanced military computer systems and datalinks. The inherently networked nature of MDA systems creates a large attack surface for potential Russian cyber weapons. This large attack surface coupled with the close operational proximity of NATO forces to Russian territory creates considerable risk for MDA datalinks and information networks.

While military networks and sensors may be resilient to some cyberspace capabilities, civilian infrastructure, vital for the safe flow of maritime traffic and operation of port facilities, is far less secure. For example, the European shipping giant Maersk reportedly lost over $300 million due to disrupted operations resulting from the Petya ransomware attack.[23] Russia could use cyber capabilities to affect regional port facilities and maritime traffic. This is particularly concerning for port facilities that the United States may use as disembarkation points in a crisis. The cyber domain is deeply interconnected to the maritime space. While this study does not fully examine how Russia's cyberspace activities may have both intended and unintended consequences for the maritime domain, enhancement and broadening of MDA capabilities will almost certainly be required to respond properly.

---

[20] Dana Goward, "Mass GPS Spoofing Attack in Black Sea?," *The Maritime Executive*, July 11, 2017, https://maritime-executive.com/editorials/mass-gps-spoofing-attack-in-black-sea.

[21] Jake Frith, "Autonomous Ships in the Baltic by 2025," *Maritime Journal*, May 24, 2017, http://www.maritimejournal.com/news101/onboard-systems/monitoring-and-control/autonomous-ships-in-the-baltic-by-2025.

[22] Joshua Davis, "Hackers Take Down the Most Wired Country in Europe," *Wired*, August 21, 2017, https://www.wired.com/2007/08/ff-estonia/.

[23] Jordan Novet, "Shipping Company Maersk Says June Cyberattack Could Cost It Up To $300 Million," CNBC, August 16, 2017, https://www.cnbc.com/2017/08/16/maersk-says-notpetya-cyberattack-could-cost-300-million.html.

Long-range Strike

The development of an effective long-range precision strike complex by Russia represents a new threat that NATO and Northern European partners are unaccustomed to countering. Since the introduction of the U.S. long-range precision strike complex in the mid-1980s, Russian military thinkers have noted the incredible potential of such systems.[24] Referred to as a reconnaissance strike complex (RSC) in Russian literature, Russian military and political leaders have been deeply unnerved by what they see as U.S. strategic nonnuclear deterrent capabilities.[25] The emerging Russian RSC has a significant naval dimension. The jewel in its crown is arguably the 3M14 Kalibr naval land attack cruise missile. Comparable to the U.S. Tomahawk, this weapon has been launched repeatedly by surface and subsurface assets operating in the Mediterranean and Caspian Seas against targets in Syria.[26] This section explains these developments in greater detail with emphasis on their implications for Western MDA.

Russia has placed considerable emphasis on its long-range strike capabilities; its future investment portfolio looks set to continue this trend. From the perspective of the Russian Navy, most new construction ships and submarines can fire land attack cruise missiles. The most significant of these are the *Yasen*-class SSN/SSGN and the prolific *Kilo*-class SSK. These attack submarines can be equipped with 40 Kalibr cruise missiles. Russia is also retrofitting existing naval assets to fire these new weapons. For example, the *Oscar II*-class SSGNs are slated to receive an upgrade that will allow them to mount 96 Kalibr cruise missiles and a *Kirov*-class CGN currently undergoing reactivation will be able to carry 80 such weapons.[27] These trends should highlight the importance of long-range strike weapons to Russian leadership and their central role in the maritime domain.

Russian thinkers write about using strategic nonnuclear strike capabilities to achieve strategic effects by targeting key adversary nodes that were previously believed to be "safe" in rear areas.[28] From a European context, this means that Russian strike capabilities are likely to target ports of disembarkation along the North Sea such as Bremerhaven, key radar installations such as the Vardo and AEGIS Ashore radars, numerous airbases, command installations, and potentially vital civilian infrastructure such as power plants. The particularly stressing aspect of this threat is that Russian platforms can conduct these strikes from a considerable distance. Depending on the range and the

---

[24] Dima P. Adamsky, "Through the Looking Glass: The Soviet Military-Technical Revolution and the American Revolution in Military Affairs," *Journal of Strategic Studies* 31, no. 2 (March 2008).

[25] James M. Acton et al., *Entanglement: Chinese and Russian Perspectives on Non-Nuclear Weapons and Nuclear Risks* (Washington, DC: Carnegie Endowment for International Peace, November 2017), http://carnegieendowment.org /2017/11/08/entanglement-chinese-and-russian-perspectives-on-non-nuclear-weapons-and-nuclear-risks-pub-73162.

[26] John Vandiver, "As Russia Launches Missiles into Syria, US Faces Strategic Dilemma," *Stars and Stripes*, June 23, 2017, https://www.stripes.com/news/as-russia-launches-missiles-into-syria-us-faces-strategic-dilemma-1.474981.

[27] Ryan Maass, "Russia to arm Antey nuclear subs with Kalibr missiles," UPI, March 7, 2017, https://www.upi.com/Russia-to-arm-Antey-nuclear-subs-with-Kalibr-missiles/6861488911868/; Tyler Rogoway, "Delivery of Russia's Refit Nuclear Battlecruiser Delayed But Progress Looks Impressive," *The War Zone*, October 31, 2017, http://www.thedrive.com/the-war-zone/15608/delivery-of-russias-refit-nuclear-battlecruiser-delayed-but-progress-looks-impressive.

[28] For examples, see: Jacob W. Kipp, *Forecasting Future War: Andrei Kokoshin and the Military-Political Debate in Contemporary Russia Andrei Kokoshin: Scholar and Bureaucrat* (Fort Leavenworth: Foreign Military Studies Office, 1999); and A.A. Kokoshin, "Strategic Stability: Scientific-Technological, Military, and Political Aspects," *Herald of the Russian Academy of Sciences,* 85.6 (2015), 472.

target, Russian vessels may be able to remain in the Barents or White Sea and still strike targets across Northern Europe.

For example, a Russian vessel equipped with a land attack cruise missile with a range of 1,500 miles could sit in the southern White Sea, wholly inside Russian territory and strike targets as far away as Belgium. A shorter-range cruise missile with a hypothetical range of 1,250 miles would allow a submarine to patrol a 220,000-square-mile area in the deep waters of the Norwegian Sea while remaining in striking range of North Sea ports. These two hypothetical ranges are roughly representative of the likely performance of the Kalibr cruise missile. Such a scenario does not consider the fact that Russia maintains a large bomber force in the Kola Peninsula and routinely deploys these assets to Kaliningrad.[29] These aircraft can carry land attack cruise missile with similar accuracy to the Kalibr and potentially greater range.[30] These new capabilities mean that the Baltic Sea, Barents Sea, Norwegian Sea, and North Sea could see considerable cruise missile traffic in a contingency scenario. This threat is totally unlike any that NATO faced during the Cold War.

Considering this challenge through the lens of MDA, several issues become apparent. First, there is a wide range of prospective launch platforms above, on, and below the surface that will need to be monitored. This includes watching port operations in Murmansk and Kaliningrad to attempt to understand weapons loadouts. A sudden change in vertical launch system (VLS) configuration to emphasize land attack weapons could be an indicator of potential military action. It will also require a new focus on forward MDA activities to monitor undersea launch platforms that can dwell in relatively protected seas. Lastly, it will require a dramatic upgrade to air surveillance and air defense capabilities. Aerial MDA radar platforms will have to be upgraded to include air moving target indicator (AMTI) capabilities to support cruise missile defense. The threat of cruise missiles transiting Swedish, Finnish, and Norwegian airspace to strike targets across Northern Europe is relatively new and underappreciated by leaders throughout the region.

Conclusion

Each of these areas represents considerable challenges to collective operations in Northern Europe. Russia is most likely to employ these capabilities in an integrated manner, significantly compounding the threat dynamic NATO and its partners face. Such actions span the totality of the littoral environment and cut across existing threat and response models employed by NATO and its partners. The expected multidomain nature of Russian activities in the Baltic and Norwegian Seas necessitates a sophisticated, integrated maritime domain awareness architecture, capable, in turn, of increasing the cost Russia would incur for coercive acts.

---

[29] Thomas Nilsen, "Strategic Bombers Striking Targets in Syria Departed from Kola," *The Independent Barents Observer,* January 30, 2016, https://thebarentsobserver.com/en/security/2016/01/strategic-bombers-striking-targets-syria-departed-kola.

[30] Kathleen H. Hicks et al., "Russian Instruments of Power," chap. 3 in *Recalibrating U.S. Strategy Toward Russia* (Washington, DC: Center for Strategic and International Studies, 2017).

Chapter 2: Maritime Domain Awareness: Today and Tomorrow

The United States is the progenitor of MDA's conceptual framework and definition. The United States defines MDA as the effective understanding of anything associated with the maritime domain that could impact the security, safety, economy, or environment of a nation or region. NATO's concept of maritime situational awareness (MSA) is largely derivative and is defined as "the understanding of military and nonmilitary events, activities and circumstance within and associated with the maritime environment that are relevant for current and future NATO operations and exercises."[31] The NATO definition highlights several important facets of MDA that are often overlooked or underemphasized. MDA is concerned with both military and nonmilitary events as well as with activities *associated* with the maritime environment. These aspects should highlight the exceptionally broad nature of MDA. This breadth dramatically increases the degree of difficulty in achieving effective MDA in contested littorals like the Baltic Sea and in multifaceted regions like the Norwegian Sea.

This chapter presents history of the MDA concept and its influence on global military and civilian thinking about the maritime domain. An analysis of the history and application of MDA reveals a key problem in how this capability is currently implemented across the global. For a number of reasons, maritime domain awareness capabilities and frameworks are overwhelmingly focused on civil maritime issues. The most stressing challenges generally discussed in the context of MDA are piracy. Yet the expansive definition of MDA coupled with the evolving threats described in Chapter 1 show how this concept must cover everything from civil operations to high-end military contingencies. In compressed geographic regions where the threat is both immediate and highly capable, a bifurcated MDA framework that creates a de facto separation between civil and military MDA capabilities will fail. A fully integrated vision and implementation of MDA, while challenging, is ultimately what is required to meet twenty-first-century maritime challenges in the Baltic Sea, Norwegian Sea, and beyond.

History

At is core, MDA is an intelligence function that seeks to develop awareness of a given domain or, in this case, set of subcomponents of the overarching maritime domain. Due to the fundamental nature of MDA to civil, law enforcement, and military operations, MDA means many things to many people. Since the beginning of seafaring, people have attempted to achieve some form of domain awareness. The invention of wireless communications created the ability to build a rudimentary common operating picture of a large area by integrating inputs from a range of platforms and sensors. During the Cold War, military awareness activities were conceived through the lens of

---

[31] Mariusz Kościelski, Ryszard K. Miler, and Mariusz Zieliński, *Maritime Situational Awareness (MSA)* (Zeszyty Naukowe Akademii Marynarki Wojennej 2007), http://www.amw.gdynia.pl/library/File/ZeszytyNaukowe/2007 /Koscielski,_Miler,_Zielinski2.pdf.

naval intelligence, were generally theater specific, and were usually oriented around two or three threats.

The modern MDA concept can be traced to the immediate aftermath of 9/11 and the concurrent explosion in information technology. The foundational document for modern MDA in the United States is Homeland Security Presidential Directive – 13 (HSPD-13) / National Security Presidential Directive–41 (NSPD-41).[32] This document, issued by President George W. Bush in 2004, created the cooperative framework needed to support MDA operations that span federal, state, and local governments as well as private companies. This document lays out six core interests for the United States to enhance the nation's security in this domain:

- *"Preventing terrorist attacks or criminal acts or hostile acts in, or the unlawful exploitation of, the Maritime Domain, and reducing the vulnerability of the Maritime Domain to such acts and exploitation;*

- *Enhancing U.S. national security and homeland security by protecting U.S. population centers, critical infrastructure, borders, harbors, ports, and coastal approaches in the Maritime Domain;*

- *Expediting recovery and response from attacks within the Maritime Domain;*

- *Maximizing awareness of security issues in the Maritime Domain in order to support U.S. forces and improve United States Government actions in response to identified threats;*

- *Enhancing international relationships and promoting the integration of U.S. allies and international and private sector partners into an improved global maritime security framework to advance common security interests in the Maritime Domain; and*

- *Ensuring seamless, coordinated implementation of authorities and responsibilities relating to the security of the Maritime Domain by and among Federal departments and agencies."*[33]

Issues of maritime security were percolating even before the issuance of this presidential directive, with President Bush remarking in a January 2002 speech that "[t]he heart of the Maritime Domain Awareness program is accurate information, intelligence, surveillance, and reconnaissance of all vessels, cargo, and people extending well beyond our traditional maritime boundaries."[34] What is plainly evident in these formulations is a focus on threats to the homeland. This is unsurprising given the overriding belief that another terrorist attack was imminent in the aftermath of 9/11. The threat of a terrorist attack that leveraged the rather porous U.S. maritime border was made all the more terrifying by the belief that such an attack vector would be ideal for some form of nuclear terrorism.[35] This was the overriding zeitgeist of the period and can be observed in other homeland

---

[32] George W. Bush, *National Security Presidential Directive NSPD-41 / Homeland Security Presidential Directive HSPD-13*, December 21, 2004, https://fas.org/irp/offdocs/nspd/nspd41.pdf.

[33] George W. Bush, *National Security Presidential Directive NSPD-41 / Homeland Security Presidential Directive HSPD-13*, December 21, 2004, https://fas.org/irp/offdocs/nspd/nspd41.pdf.

[34] Steven C. Boraz, "Maritime Domain Awareness: Myths and Realities," *Naval War College Review* 62, no. 3 (2009), https://www.hsdl.org/?abstract&did=699259.

[35] U.S. Department of Homeland Security, *National Plan to Achieve Maritime Domain Awareness, for the Nation Strategy for Maritime Security*, October 2005, https://www.dhs.gov/sites/default/files/publications/HSPD_MDAPlan_0.pdf.

security-focused decisions of the period such as the procurement of the large unmanned aircraft (UAS) for U.S. Customs and Border Patrol.[36] This homeland security focus would become ingrained in the MDA community and reinforced by future trends in the security environment.

HSPD-13/NSPD-41 set in motion a series actions within the interagency. The core piece of this effort was the *National Strategy for Maritime Security,* which in turn beget a series of implementation plans, including the *National Plan to Achieve Maritime Domain Awareness.*[37] These documents form the backbone for the modern U.S. system of MDA and are still referenced widely today. From an organizational perspective, the post–9/11 era also led to the creation of the National Maritime Intelligence Center (NMIC) to serve as an MDA fusion center.[38] This organization is run by the U.S. Navy with considerable support from the U.S. Coast Guard. Because of the close relationship between homeland security and law enforcement operations, the MDA mission has been fully embraced by the U.S. Coast Guard. Following 9/11, the priorities for the U.S. Navy quickly shifted overseas to support Operation Enduring Freedom and subsequently Operation Iraqi Freedom.

The relationship between law enforcement and MDA was also the result of the considerable and ongoing U.S. experience in the Caribbean. The Joint Interagency Task Force – South (JIATF-South) is, in many ways, a model for achieving effective MDA in a collaborative environment.[39] This group dates back to the 1980s when the "War on Drugs" was the dominant paradigm for responding to illegal drugs in the United States.[40] This organization was created to bring together the wide array of international, federal, state, and local actors with responsibility for illicit trafficking in the Caribbean basin. The success of JIATF-South in interdicting illicit maritime traffic in this region served as a model of how successful cooperation in the maritime domain can work across jurisdictions and was the first to effectively bring together military and law enforcement capabilities. However, the core law enforcement mission of JIAFT-South only further emphasizes the law enforcement and homeland security aspects of MDA.

The history of MDA would not be complete without discussing the rise of the automatic identification system (AIS) for vessel tracking. AIS regularly transmits a ship's position and heading as well as ship identification information via VHF radio.[41] The shipboard VHF transceiver also receives the AIS transmissions of nearby vessels and generates a nearby operational picture. Since 2002, AIS has been required on all vessels over 300 gross tons by the International Maritime Organization (IMO).[42] Many smaller vessels also carry AIS transceivers for safety reasons. This technology has dramatically improved the ability of users of the maritime domain to conduct safe operations with due regard for other maritime traffic.

---

[36] Interviews with former U.S. government officials.

[37] U.S. Department of Homeland Security, *National Plan to Achieve Maritime Domain Awareness, for the Nation Strategy for Maritime Security.*

[38] Interviews with maritime domain awareness experts.

[39] Interviews with maritime intelligence experts.

[40] Evan Munsing and Christopher J. Lamb, "Joint Interagency Task Force-South: The Best Known, Least Understood Interagency Success," *Institute for National Strategic Studies, Strategic Perspectives*, no. 5, http://ndupress.ndu.edu /Portals/68/Documents/stratperspective/inss/Strategic-Perspectives-5.pdf.

[41] Interviews with maritime domain awareness experts.

[42] "Automatic Identification Systems (AIS)," *International Maritime Organization*, http://www.imo.org/en/OurWork/safety /navigation/pages/ais.aspx.

However, AIS is not without its drawbacks. Creating a unified operational picture across a broad environment required linking together multiple terrestrial AIS receivers given the inherently limited range of VHF radio systems. Creating a unified European maritime operating picture was one of the major triumphs of U.S. Naval Forces Europe (NAVEUR) during the mid-2000s. Under the leadership of Admiral Henry Ulrich and then-Vice Admiral Sandy Winnefeld, members of the NAVEUR staff were instrumental in the creation of a common operating picture that drew heavily on AIS data feeds. This program grew and became the Maritime Safety and Security Information Systems (MSSIS) that has been adopted globally to facilitate unclassified data sharing.[43]

MSSIS exponentially increased the amount of data available for analysts and operators. However, it is an inherently unclassified network primarily designed for civil and law enforcement operators. Adding classified information or information sources to this common operating picture would dramatically increase its utility but is often not possible due to sharing limitations. Issues of data sharing are further complicated by firewalls that often exist between military and law enforcement authorities and Five-Eyes, NATO, and NATO partner sharing arrangements.

More recently, AIS receivers have been placed on satellites enabling a truly global maritime picture.[44] Prior to the introduction of a space sensor layer, AIS had been limited to coastal receivers. Several commercial operators provide freely available AIS maps with additional data layers available for paying customers. These services are in high demand by civil maritime firms, such as shipping lines and port operators.

AIS has been a massive boon to civil and government operators alike. Its utility has been further increased by combining it with cargo-tracking agreements such as the Container Security Initiative and global information exchanges such as the Global Integrated Shipping Information System. The creation of a global MDA framework for commercial vessels creates major benefits for monitoring illicit trafficking. This has proved especially useful in enforcing sanctions regimes and countering North Korea's weapons proliferation network.

The utility and ubiquity of AIS has created a dangerous side effect especially among smaller nations. Due to the incredible coverage this technology provides, nations have divested of more traditional maritime domain awareness technologies. This introduces the prospect of a single point of failure in their overall MDA capability that could be exploited. Because AIS relies on returning accurate data from vessels, it cannot capture noncooperative targets, including those who choose not to broadcast or those who are deliberately spoofing their ship data.

Maritime Domaine Awareness Today

Recently, there are some indications that elements of the U.S. military are pushing toward a holistic vision of MDA that would better capture military requirements often lost in civilian-centered MDA formulations. The recently released *Littoral Operations in a Contested Environment,* a U.S. Navy / Marine Corps operating concept, offers a wholly integrated vision for future naval operations in

---

[43] Interviews with maritime domain awareness experts.
[44] European Space Agency, "Telecommunications & Integrated Applications: Satellite – Automatic Identification System (SAT-AIS)," http://www.esa.int/Our_Activities/Telecommunications_Integrated_Applications/Satellite_-_Automatic_Identification_System_SAT-AIS.

complex environments like the Baltic Sea.[45] The new operating concept places effective understanding of the entire maritime operating environment at the heart of its proposed intelligence capability. Notably, it calls for a comprehensive understanding of the entire maritime domain, integrating threats across the spectrum of concern. The thrust toward inclusivity of stressing military threats is driven in part by the global proliferation of advanced military technologies, namely antiship cruise missiles. For the U.S. Marine Corps in particular, which concerns itself with the potential for amphibious operations, there are few places that can today be described as permissive operating environments.

The overriding practice of MDA has heavily focused on the civil, law enforcement, and homeland security elements of the maritime domain. The effect of this implicit intellectual paradigm is that MDA becomes a distinct function divorced from high-end warfighting. In practice, this creates one network of sensors, platforms, information-sharing agreements, fusion centers, governance regimes, etc., for MDA and a separate network that includes kinetic response operations necessary for warfighting.

A bifurcated paradigm makes a degree of sense from a U.S. perspective. The United States developed the MDA model in the wake of 9/11 primarily to address threats beyond "traditional" military lanes. At the same time, the United States was not worried about state-level naval threats to the homeland. In fact, the United States has not seriously considered this threat since the 1970s and 1980s.[46] As discussed in the previous section, the overwhelming focus of HSPD-13/NSPD-41 was on homeland security. At the same time, the European concept of MSA was built upon the U.S. definition of the challenge, placed within the context of rising of illicit traffic in the Mediterranean, and couched in a belief that Europe would be a net security exporter.

The focus on improving information sharing in the civil and law enforcement spaces makes considerable sense when considering the impediments to real information sharing and operational collaboration at a level where sharing classified military data is a prerequisite. The degree of difficulty with respect to data sharing is heightened by the number of distinct actors that contribute to MDA in this region. This includes NATO, the European Union, regional cooperative agreements, national-level military and law enforcement agencies, and civil operators. The complexity would be made more manageable if a single nation had the jurisdiction and resources required to address the requirements for effective MDA. However, this neat hypothetical is not the reality facing policymakers in any of the major global complex maritime environments.[47]

A comprehensive approach to MDA is vital. The existing maritime enterprise will need to adapt to the reality that growing technological advancements and lowered barriers to its diffusion will provide an array of state and nonstate actors with the means to field sophisticated systems to either avoid detection or directly strike targets. The JIATF-South experience may again be

---

[45] U.S. Department of the Navy, *Littoral Operations in a Contested Environment*, 2017, https://marinecorpsconceptsandprograms.com/sites/default/files/concepts/pdf-uploads /LOCE%20full%20size%20edition.pdf.

[46] There is an argument that the U.S. Navy has enduring force-protection requirements for Kings Bay, Georgia, and Bangor, Washington. However, these are of a fundamentally different tenor than broad awareness requirements for confronting naval threats along the entire U.S. coastline.

[47] This term can be accurately applied to the East China Sea, South China Sea, Baltic Sea, Mediterranean Sea, Gulf of Aden, Persian Gulf, and Artic Sea.

instructive. This task force had to adapt its tactics, techniques, and procedures to prosecute a new generation of neutrally buoyant and fully submersible craft used for illicit trafficking. These developments highlight the need to conceive of MDA as an activity that must seek to understand the environment from seafloor to space.

The Baltic Sea and Norwegian Sea each serve as unique case studies in the evolving nature of modern MDA activities. In the Baltic Sea, the threat is heightened by the region's complex geography and short distances. This means that capabilities are easy to hide and response times are likely to be very short. The Norwegian Sea demonstrates the need to fully integrate ASW operations into the broader conceptual framework of MDA. The marriage of exceptionally quiet submarines with precise long-range strike weapons is a new maritime issue that NATO must confront. The following sections explore these basin specific issues and their consequences in greater detail.

Complex Maritime Environments and Geographic Compression

The Baltic Sea is the definition of a complex maritime environment, creating significant challenges for both civil and military operators Environmentally, this sea has large differences in depth, radical challenges in salinity, and a pronounced temperature gradient. This creates a difficult environment for acoustic sensors. Geographically, the sea is dotted with numerous islands adding to the maritime "clutter."

From a use perspective, the Baltic Sea is one of the most traveled bodies of water in the world. The shipping density approaches that of the Strait of Malacca. Furthermore, approximately 3 million barrels of petroleum products transit the Danish Straits every day.[48] This is in addition to the massive Nord Stream pipeline that carries natural gas from Russia to Germany. The Baltic Sea neatly fits Milan Vego's definition of a narrow sea where "narrow seas are characterized by the presence of large number of friendly, enemy, and neutral commercial vessels, warships, and auxiliaries."[49] This combination of factors makes the accurate assessment of the maritime domain exceptionally challenging.

The compressed threat geography of the Baltic Sea region creates further challenges for achieving effective MDA. Put simply, Russia is actively operating in this region daily from adjacent territory meaning that potentially provocative operations can be carried out with little to no warning. Additionally, the Kaliningrad enclave serves as a forward blocking position for Russian military forces. This is what is meant by geographic compression. Compression is furthered by the introduction of long-range standoff strike weapons that can hit rear area sanctuaries. Even if the Baltic Sea region is not the target of such weapons, its airspace will be transited by these weapons in a contingency scenario. The region's geography makes this threat inescapable.

Cyberspace supercharges the compression dynamic, rendering physical geography less relevant than ever before. An individual halfway around the world can impact the safe operations of ships in the Baltic Sea. The cyberspace domain also creates new threat vectors with which MDA must

---

[48] Lejla Villar and Marson Hamilton, "The Danish and Turkish Straits are critical to Europe's crude oil and petroleum trade," U.S. Energy Information Administration.
[49] Milan Vego, "On Littoral Warfare," *Naval War College Review* 68, no. 2 (2015), https://usnwc2.usnwc.edu /getattachment/fe330f71-6933-457d-890d-a19726bb508c/On-Littoral-Warfare.aspx.

contend. While the cyber aspects of the maritime domain are a study unto themselves, it is vital to acknowledge the severity of the threat posed by malign state and nonstate cyber actors to the maritime domain.

The reality of geographic compression is not new in the broad Baltic Sea region. For example, Finland has long had to contend with its long land border with Russia. The reality of this phenomenon is only now being appreciated by a wide array of regional states. For example, the Swedish Defense Committee recently released a report calling for the recommitment of Sweden to the total defense concept. This document contains some stark findings about Sweden's likely position in a full-scale contingency scenario concluding that electrical power is likely to be very limited, food will be rationed, fuel stocks will be greatly stressed, and the medical system may be unable to keep up with the strain.[50] This is a much different picture of the implications of military action than was present during the Cold War where such rear area and civilian functions were perceived to be more sheltered from attack.[51]

In practice, what does complexity and geographic compression mean for MDA? Taking the Baltic Sea as a case study, the platforms, networks, and people needed for ensuring safe operation of the Baltic maritime sector are, in almost all cases, the same that will have to respond in stressing contingency scenarios. An aerial MDA aircraft equipped with an advanced maritime search radar should have the ability to not only feed into a regional MDA fusion center that is developing the regional common operating picture. This same aircraft needs to cue antiship cruise missiles should the need arise in a relatively seamless manner. A fully implemented, scalable MDA architecture would also integrate regional air and missile defense capabilities, increasingly important as the cruise missile threat increases. The bottom line is that MDA and battlespace awareness cannot be viewed as separate concepts; rather, one must conceptualize maritime domain awareness as flowing seamlessly from monitoring civil traffic to conducting missile defense operations.

What Happened to ASW

This discussion thus far has overwhelmingly focused on the surface dimension of MDA activities while touching on some of the issues that bring the aerial sub-component into this concept. The undersea aspect of MDA has not yet been explored. This can be attributed, in part, to the fact that undersea warfare has been largely kept intellectually separate from MDA. Historically, the threats emanating from the undersea domain have been captured under antisubmarine warfare (ASW) and its associated doctrine. The distinction between MDA and ASW is understandable given the differences between surface and subsurface operations. However, a holistic vision of MDA must account for the undersea domain to include ASW as well as related undersea warfare regimes.

The split between MDA and ASW is understandable because of the history of both concepts as well as some key differences in the dynamics of these operations. The recent nature of the MDA concept contrasts strongly with the 70-plus-year history of ASW and its community of interest. The threat posed by adversary submarines is also more concrete and immediate than those

---

[50] The Swedish Defence Commission secretariat, *Resilience: The Total Defence Concept and the Development of Civil Defence 2021–2025,* http://www.government.se/4afeb9/globalassets/government/dokument/forsvarsdepartementet /resilience---report-summary---20171220ny.pdf.

[51] This assumes a conventional conflict. In the case of a nuclear war, such assumptions are rendered moot.

considered under the MDA umbrella. The immediacy of the threat also has a historical element. During the Cold War, ASW was one of the primary missions for NATO navies. Soviet submarines were one of the two primary threat vectors for the Soviet Union in the maritime domain. (The other was long-range naval aviation with antiship cruise missiles.) Given these facts, it is no surprise that ASW developed in a robust and integrated manner given the severity of the threat.

The distinction between the concepts may also be explained by some key differences between the sensors and platforms required for successful ASW and those that contribute to MDA. Speaking generically, all ASW platforms and sensors can contribute to the MDA mission but not all MDA platforms and sensors can contribute to the ASW mission. The need to carry a large payload of sonobuoys combined with specialized acoustic processing equipment creates certain design requirements for ASW-capable maritime patrol aircraft. This specialization extends to the aircrews and command staffs that operate these platforms. ASW operators will naturally want their aircraft performing their primary mission rather than other tasks. The need for specialization among personnel can also make it more challenging to fully achieve multimission capability.

MDA was conceived at a point in time when the threat of undersea warfare was low. Russia was a pale shadow of its Cold War past and China was a nascent naval power. This reality coupled with the post–9/11 focus on homeland security and nonstate threats meant that ASW and MDA continued on two separate tracks. The inherent specialization required of ASW operators and many of its platforms created a further barrier for the integration of ASW into a comprehensive MDA approach. However, there are other areas of undersea warfare, beyond countering adversary submarines, that showcase the need for an integrated approach.

Chapter 2 discussed the new and severe threat posed by Russian submarines with advanced, conventional long-range cruise missiles. These vessels are likely to operate in and around the Norwegian Sea given it is a favorable area for submarine operations. For MDA, the result is that previously distinct missions such as ASW and air defense will have to work hand in hand. Understanding submarine deployments and their operational patterns can help inform the placement of a variety of air defense capabilities. At the same time, air defense operators could provide key cueing information to ASW platforms in a crisis scenario.

Understanding the subsurface dimension of the maritime domain is not limited to ASW. Mine warfare is a considerable concern in the Baltic Sea region. Even without the emplacement of new mines, the Baltic Sea is thought to contain over 50 million pieces of unexploded ordinance, relics of twentieth-century conflicts.[52] This relatively shallow basin replete with natural chokepoints is an excellent venue for mine warfare. This only adds to the basin's complexity. While the capabilities required to confront the mine warfare threat are quite distinct from ASW systems, the understanding of the environment required for successful ASW and counter-mine missions is similar. Submarines can be used to emplace sea mines creating additional linkages between ASW and mine warfare.

Combat swimmers and amphibious special forces further the interrelationship between the undersea domain and maritime domain awareness. The threat posed by these forces was

---

[52] Carsten Holm, "German Waters Teeming with WWII Munitions," *Spiegel Online*, April 11, 2013, http://www.spiegel.de /international/germany/dangers-of-unexploded-wwii-munitions-in-north-and-baltic-seas-a-893113.html.

discussed at length in Chapter 1. The capabilities needed to perceive and react to this threat are closely related to ASW, especially in a littoral environment such as the Baltic Sea region. The threat posed to undersea cables by Russian submarines and other capabilities similarly falls into this category and has relevance in the Baltic and Norwegian seas.

These threat vectors demonstrate how undersea warfare is far more than ASW. However, the sensors, platforms, and expertise needed for ASW will be valuable in countering these threats. At the same time, the growing threat of submarine-launched cruise missiles means that ASW efforts will have to be closely correlated with missile defense efforts. Early tracks from missile defense sensors may provide ASW assets with valuable targeting information and enable rapid prosecution of adversary launch platforms. Inversely, cueing data from ASW missions may help better position missile defense sensors and interceptors to track and kill adversary missiles. This connection between ASW and MDA is most pronounced in the North Atlantic littoral and the Norwegian Sea as these are the likely cruise missile launch points for Russian nuclear-powered submarines with considerably greater magazine depth than the *Kilo*-class submarines Russia has, to date, used for land attack missions.

These threats show how important the undersea domain is to an integrated understanding of the entire maritime domain. While past practices established ASW as a mission apart, a twenty-first-century approach to the threats emanating from the maritime domain must embrace the inherent complexity of the sub-components of the overall domain.

A Vision for the Future

A holistic approach to MDA that directly links collection capabilities to response options is needed to meet twenty-first-century threats in the Baltic and Norwegian seas. One must avoid the common trap that "[a]ll too often, collecting information becomes an end in itself."[53] The true value of an MDA architecture is not in the amount of data it collects but in its ability to provide policymakers with timely, relevant, and accurate information that assists officials to make difficult political decisions. In contested maritime environments, adversary states will seek to impede clarity, employing strategies that seek both to leverage the natural ambiguity of the maritime domain and to create additional ambiguity, such as by employing hybrid tactics. The MDA architecture in the Baltic Sea and Norwegian Sea basins must be capable of meeting policymakers' needs under the most challenging conditions. It should also be scalable to provide capabilities across a wide range of scenarios from law enforcement to surface warfare.

Using the collection, analysis, action framework, a twenty-first-century MDA capability can be described as follows:

- *Collection:* Sensors must capture inputs from the undersea, surface, and aerial sub-components of the overarching maritime domain. Sensors should be multimission where possible. Coverage should be scalable to reflect peacetime constraints and wartime

---

[53] Milan Vego, "On Littoral Warfare," *Naval War College Review* 68, no. 2 (2015), https://usnwc2.usnwc.edu /getattachment/fe330f71-6933-457b-890d-a19726bb508c/On-Littoral-Warfare.aspx.

requirements. This scalability will necessitate forces that can rapidly constitute in periods of crisis.

- *Analysis:* Data gathered by sensors must be fused and analyzed by trained human operators with a keen understanding of specific regional dynamics and patterns of activity. Automated technologies can dramatically augment human operators but cannot replace the insights they are able to derive. This additional value is a key component of effective MDA.

- *Action:* Data and intelligence products are useless unless they can be disseminated to a broad range of consumers in a timely manner. An MDA network must move raw and processed data between a range of platforms to include submarines. Such a network will require both technical solutions to protect it from nonkinetic attacks and political frameworks to move sensitive data among relevant contributors to regional MDA capabilities.

Chapter 3: Regional Capabilities

Western nations operating in the Baltic Sea and Norwegian Sea host a range of capabilities relevant to the region's MDA challenge. This includes systems designed for civilian and military missions that are operated by ministries of defense, interior, and justice. This chapter assesses these capabilities in light of the threat context presented in Chapters 1 and 2. In turn, this gap analysis informs the recommendations made in Chapter 4.

The steady-state assessment of current and projected Western capabilities uses the collection, analysis, and action framework introduced in Chapter 2. This assessment is done on a basin-specific basis to reflect the unique requirements in each region. Assessment of collection systems is done on a country-by-country basis and subdivided into aerial, surface, and subsurface given the technical distinctions between these collection regimes. Analysis and action are discussed in a more holistic manner in keeping with the integrated nature of these functions. The basin-specific discussions subdivide analysis into data integration and data analysis while action is split into operations and resiliency.

Baltic Sea

The major gap in the Baltic Sea is a lack of integration across the northern European "seam." The fact that Sweden and Finland are outside NATO creates persistent issues for achieving an integrated MDA capability. Potential mitigating approaches heavily leverage improving bilateral relationships and the potential resident in Germany's Baltic Maritime Component Command (BMCC). Additional gaps include an inability to integrate a range of aerial, surface, and subsurface information to achieve a unified picture of the maritime domain. This issue is only furthered by the need to include a robust understanding of the land domain given the relatively small size of the Baltic Sea. A land force, equipped with antiship or antiaircraft weapons could deny the use of this sea in a relatively easy manner. The nature of a littoral sea dramatically increases the degree of difficulty for achieving effective MDA.

Collection

When considering collection capabilities, the region is relatively well equipped with regards to air surveillance but more challenged in the surface or subsurface domains. The gaps in these areas are primarily driven by the geography of the Baltic Sea region, need to accurately perceive potentially deceptive Russian actions, potential for electronic or cyber warfare degradation of sensors, and requirements for detecting small submerged targets.

Aerial

Germany maintains a robust air surveillance capability based on Ground Master 400 radar system deployed in fixed sites around the country.[54] This enterprise ground-based surveillance capability is paired with the Patriot air defense system. Germany plans to replace its aging Patriot system with the Medium Extended Air Defense System (MEADS), which incorporates the latest Patriot interceptors with new radars and command systems.[55] This system's radar enhancements compared to the existing Patriot system is noteworthy. This ground-based capability is augmented by several classes of naval vessels with varying degrees of air surveillance capability. The most capable of which is the F124 *Saschen*-class air defense frigate incorporating the common Thales Nederland SMART-L surveillance radar and Airborne Phased Array (APAR) tracking and acquisition radar along with U.S. vertical-launch systems.[56] These capabilities, if composited, provide the German military a significant air surveillance capability both over its own littorals and potentially further into the Baltic Sea. However, it is unclear how effectively Germany can integrate its ground and sea-based sensors. In addition, the future addition of MEADS remains in doubt with the development of this system plagued by delays and cost overruns.[57]

Poland operates a fixed ground-based air surveillance capability RAT-31 DL radar system. The procurement of these radars was funded by NATO's Security Investment Program, with the radars operated as part of NATO's system of long-range air surveillance radars.[58] Poland is planning on developing a deployable, mobile air defense system and has recently decided on the latest version of the Patriot system with some additional enhancements. However, this procurement program will not reach initial operational capability until the mid-2020s. In addition, the United States and Poland continue to negotiate over the final price of these systems and what additional capabilities will be incorporated.[59] Poland's current capability, while adequate for current missions, will not support Polish ambitions. Although Polish officials acknowledge this gap, there are ongoing concerns about the total costs of several planned acquisition programs.[60] In addition, political considerations about domestic production have dramatically slowed several key defense programs.[61]

---

[54] "German Air Force commissions first TRS Ground Master 400 radar," *Air Force Technology,* November 5, 2013, https://www.airforce-technology.com/news/newsgerman-air-force-commissions-first-trs-ground-master-400-radar/.
[55] Andrea Shalal, "Germany aims to finish missile defense deal with MBDA, Lockheed by year end: ministry," Reuters, June 20, 2017, https://www.reuters.com/article/us-airshow-paris-germany-meads/germany-aims-to-finish-missile-defense-deal-with-mbda-lockheed-by-year-end-ministry-idUSKBN19B2OJ.
[56] Stephen Saunders, *IHS Jane's Fighting Ships 2016–2017* (London: IHS Jane's, 2015), 267.
[57] Shalal, "Germany aims to finish missile defense deal with MBDA."
[58] M. Samseer, "Selex delivers three air defence radars to Poland," *Airforce Technology,* October 11, 2015, http://www.airforce-technology.com/news/newsselex-delivers-three-air-defence-radars-to-poland-4690357/.
[59] Jen Judson, "Poland has sticker shock over 'unacceptable' price tag for Patriot buy," *Defense News,* December 6, 2017, https://www.defensenews.com/land/2017/12/06/poland-surprised-by-high-price-tag-for-its-long-awaited-patriot-purchase/.
[60] Judson, "Poland has sticker shock"; and Jacek Siminski, "Polish Air Force Further Postpones Procurement of 5th Generation Fighters to Replace MIG-29 and SU-22 Jets," *The Aviationist*, November 28, 2016, https://theaviationist.com/2016/11/28/polish-air-force-further-postpones-procurement-of-5th-generation-fighters-to-replace-mig-29-and-su-22-jets/.
[61] Emily Tamkin, "What Is Happening to Poland's Military?," *Foreign Policy*, January 5, 2017, http://foreignpolicy.com/2017/01/05/what-is-happening-to-polands-military/; and Dominic Perry, "Airbus Helicopters intensifies compensation fight with Poland," *FlightGlobal*, January 2, 2018, https://www.flightglobal.com/news/articles/airbus-helicopters-intensifies-compensation-fight-wi-444551/.

Denmark's ground-based air surveillance capability centers on the RAC 3D radar, a target acquisition and tracking radar rather than an enterprise air surveillance radar.[62] The RAC 3D radar has a roughly 100-km range in comparison to the 300-plus-km range of an enterprise system. This modest ground-based capability is paired with a significant air surveillance and defense capability from naval platforms. The three *Iver Huitfeldt*-class FFGs mount the same excellent radar system as the German F124 frigates.[63] The overall capability portfolio, if integrated, makes considerable sense. However, Denmark has not acquired long-range SAMs for these vessels and the integration of its sea-based and land-based sensors for air surveillance is unclear. Denmark is surrounded on three sides by water, roughly 170 km across at its widest point. However, the sufficiency of its naval forces to monitor and protect the Danish Straits may be dramatically curtailed if Danish FFGs are tasked to support NATO ballistic missile defense (BMD) missions.

Sweden is one of a few European nations that operate an indigenous airborne early warning and control (AEW&C) aircraft. Its three S-100 Argus aircraft are equipped with a powerful AESA "balance beam" radar.[64] This airborne layer provides considerable coverage against a wide array of targets. However, the small number of platforms means that the overall capability is highly constrained. Sweden's ground-based radar systems and air defense capabilities are being upgraded with the procurement of the U.S. Patriot system scheduled for delivery in the early 2020s.[65] This will dramatically improve Sweden's capabilities and symbolizes the improving defense relationship between Sweden and NATO. Despite these capabilities and planned improvements, it is unclear the extent to which Swedish air surveillance and defense capabilities are integrated and postured against likely Russian threats, especially those coming from the Kola Peninsula. Also, recent air intrusions highlight capacity shortcomings to respond quickly to provocations.[66]

Finland operates the GM 400 radar for its ground-based air surveillance capability. However, unlike other European nations they operate mobile air surveillance radars. This is unsurprising given their proximity to Russia and the inherent vulnerability of fixed ground-based systems.[67] Finland does not possess a robust naval air surveillance capability, but this may change with the next-generation Finnish corvette / frigate. While this vessel is still in the design phases and not slated for service until the mid- to late 2020s, early indications are that it would possess increased air warfare capabilities.[68] Finland's ground-based air defense capabilities include the second-generation Norwegian Advanced Surface to Air Missile System (NASAMS 2) and the mobile Sentinel X band radar.[69] The high mobility of this system is unsurprising given Finnish operational requirements. Finland's capability mix reflects the Finnish military strategy of defensive operations aimed at

[62] "RAC 3D," *Deagel*, accessed February 7, 2018, http://www.deagel.com/Tactical-Vehicles/RAC-3D_a000466001.aspx.

[63] Saunders, *IHS Jane's Fighting Ships 2016–2017*, 200.

[64] International Institute for Strategic Studies (IISS), *Military Balance 2017*, 163, https://www.iiss.org/en/publications /military%20balance/issues/the-military-balance-2017-b47b; and "Finland Updating its Air Defense Systems," *Defense Industry Daily*, January 26, 2014, https://www.iiss.org/en/publications/military%20balance/issues/the-military-balance-2017-b47b/mb2017-04-europe-2-9e8c.

[65] Johannes Hellstrom and Mike Stone, "Sweden seeks to buy $1 billion U.S. Patriot air defense missile system," Reuters, November 7, 2017, https://www.reuters.com/article/us-sweden-defense-raytheon/sweden-seeks-to-buy-1-billion-u-s-patriot-air-defense-missile-system-idUSKBN1D72WM.

[66] "Russian jets practiced attacks on Sweden," *The Local*, April 22, 2013, https://www.thelocal.se/20130422/47474.

[67] "Finland receives new radar," UPI, January 16, 2013, https://www.upi.com/Finland-receives-new-radar /25091358365959/.

[68] Interviews with Finnish security experts.

[69] IISS, *Military Balance 2017*, 163.

attriting potential adversaries. In addition, Finland is considerably vulnerable to electronic and cyber warfare capabilities due to its proximity to Russia.

The Baltic states all maintain considerable air surveillance capability, far beyond what might be for states their size. These investments have been primarily funded by NATO as part of the BALTNET air defense capability, which integrates into the larger NATO Integrated Air and Missile Defense System (NATINAMDS). Estonia operates the same GM 400 radars as Finland, having participated in a joint procurement program.[70] These radars are mobile but are generally deployed in fixed locations. Latvia operates several TPS-77 enterprise search radars and four mobile Sentinel systems. Latvia currently is taking delivery of three upgraded TPS-77 MRR systems that provide a mobile search radar capability.[71] Lithuania is building three new fixed radar sites to support the overall BALTNET capability and replace aging Soviet-era radar systems.[72] The exact air surveillance radar it has deployed is unclear, but the overall performance is likely similar to systems operated by the other Baltic states. Collectively this air surveillance capability is substantial, but it is unclear how it would perform in a heavily degraded EW environment. Furthermore, the fixed nature of several of these systems makes them especially vulnerable to long-range fires to include precision rocket artillery.

Surface

While each nation has distinct surface capabilities and shortcomings to contribute to MDA, all are over-reliant on AIS for monitoring the maritime domain. As discussed previously, AIS is a fantastic technology that dramatically improves the safety at sea. However, it can become a crutch for nations seeking to understand and protect the maritime commons. AIS can be spoofed, jammed, or simply turned off. Nations have become over-reliant on AIS systems for managing maritime traffic.[73] This is a major problem in the Baltic Sea where AIS is key for controlling a huge volume of ships. It is highly plausible that this reliance on AIS could be exploited by a malicious actor to create confusion or conceal activities. AIS is a powerful tool but it must be paired with active collection from a range of sensors and integrated analysis to understand the entire surface maritime environment. This approach enables the identification of vessels that are either hiding among the AIS clutter or are not what they are claiming to be.

Germany operates a considerable surface naval force to include the new K130 corvettes for operations in littoral waters.[74] Germany also maintains several coast guard vessels for law enforcement activities. However, the German Coast Guard is not a unitary institution; instead it is a collection of several relevant agencies. This can further create organizational and institutional challenges for achieving a unified MDA capability.[75] These surface assets are supplemented by P-

[70] "Estonian Air Force commissions TRS' GM 400 air defence radar," *Airforce Technology*, March 26, 2013, https://www.airforce-technology.com/news/newsestonian-air-force-trs-gm-400-defence-radar/.
[71] James Drew, "Lockheed Nears Delivery of Latvia's TPS-77 MRR Radar," *Aviation Week Network*, October 13, 2017, http://aviationweek.com/awindefense/lockheed-nears-delivery-latvia-s-tps-77-mrr-radar.
[72] Republic of Lithuania, "Construction begins at two radar posts as Lithuania enhances air defence surveillance," Ministry of National Defence, September 25, 2015, http://kam.lt/en/news_1098/current_issues /constructions_begin_in_two_radiolocation_posts_as_lithuania_enhances_airspace_surveillance.
[73] Interviews with Baltic security experts.
[74] Saunders, *IHS Jane's Fighting Ships 2016–2017*, 298.
[75] Interviews with Baltic security experts.

3C Orion maritime patrol aircraft (MPA) as well as NH90 and Lynx naval helicopters.[76] Germany's fleet of Type 212 submarines can also provide meaningful contributions in this regard. All together, these platforms provide a considerable level of capability for the German Navy to understand the maritime environment. However, the German military is facing an across-the-board readiness challenge that hampers the overall capacity of German forces.[77] This is particularly concerning for steady-state missions in the Baltic Sea.

Poland does not have considerable capabilities in this domain. In the overall context of Polish defense priorities, the navy is not a focus area. An integrated surface search capability is further challenged by the poor current state of the Polish Navy, a mix of Soviet and Western systems, and challenges in the procurement system. For example, Poland planned to procure seven large corvettes of the *Gawron*-class.[78] This program was canceled with the first ship unfinished. Presently, Poland is planning to procure several small to medium-sized patrol vessels as well as a range of unmanned systems.[79] The planned capabilities of these vessels are well aligned with the operational requirements of the region. Unmanned systems can help the small Polish Navy maximize its overall capacity. However, the ability of the Polish government to execute this plan is unclear given ongoing issues with defense procurement. At the same time, Poland has considerable requirements for surface surveillance due to its proximity to Kaliningrad.

Denmark maintains land-based radar coverage of the Danish Straits and surrounding waters. This is operated by the Danish Defense Forces and data is supplied to the Danish Maritime Assistance Service, a component of the nation's military operations center.[80] While Denmark has a small naval force that is arguably designed for expeditionary operations, the overall capability portfolio, if integrated, makes considerable sense. Coast guard functions are also assigned to the Defense Forces. Denmark's terrestrial surface search radars, while sufficient for maintaining the safe operation of the Danish maritime commons, are likely inadequate. Note that Danish collection capabilities against both surface and aerial targets is likely to expand dramatically in the coming years with the acquisition of the F-35 Joint Strike Fighter. While this represents a huge collection capability, it is unclear if Denmark can adequately handle the data produced by this platform. This "data glut" will be discussed in the subsequent analysis section.

Sweden maintains a series of coastal radars to monitor its massive coastline. However, this radar system is inherently limited both by weather and by the region's complex maritime geography. The archipelagic nature of the Stockholm maritime area inherently limits the efficacy of ground-based systems. The geography of the Baltic Sea near Gotland is more conducive to coastal radar systems. However, coastal radars have a limited range and may not be able to detect low-signature targets.

---

[76] IISS, *Military Balance 2017*, 117–18.

[77] Rick Noack, "Afraid of a major conflict? The German military is currently unavailable," *Washington Post*, January 24, 2018, https://www.washingtonpost.com/news/worldviews/wp/2018/01/24/afraid-of-a-major-conflict-the-german-military-is-currently-unavailable/?utm_term=.d50d3a984b54.

[78] "Former corvette re-launched as re-designated OPV," *Poland at Sea*, July 2, 2015, http://www.polandatsea.com/former-corvette-re-launched-as-re-designated-opv/.

[79] Jaroslaw Adamowski, "Subs, cruise missiles to drive Poland's Navy modernization," *Defense News,* August 28, 2017, https://www.defensenews.com/smr/european-balance-of-power/2017/08/28/subs-cruise-missiles-to-drive-polands-navy-modernization/.

[80] Stine Skouby Asnæs et al., *Technological Assessment on the Possibility of Shore Based Pilotage in Danish Waters* (Lyngby: COWI, 2014), http://www.balticpilotage.org/files/bpac%20-%20report%20-%20shore%20based%20pilotage%20-%2028.05.2015.pdf.

The Swedish Navy is designed for this environment, albeit it with a limited capacity. The Visby Class corvettes are designed for stealth and equipped with Towed Array Sonar (TAS) and Variable-Depth Sonar (VDS), making them capable of performing a variety of surface and subsurface monitoring functions.[81] The Swedish submarine force can help to provide surface monitoring through acoustic tracking. This collection approach has considerable benefits for understanding Russian operational patterns and habits. Sweden operates three maritime patrol aircraft based on the Bombadier Dash-8.[82] However, these aircraft are operated by the Swedish Coast Guard, an agency under the Ministry of Justice rather than the Ministry of Defence.[83] There are concerns that these aircraft, a vital capability for understanding the maritime domain, are not manned at an adequate level and may not have the capacity required by the threat environment.

Finland faces many of the same challenges as Sweden but has both a more complex geographic area and a smaller force. Monitoring the Aland Islands is a particularly vexing problem for any force, with some 60 inhabited islands and 6,500 total islands in the archipelago.[84] The Finnish Navy is a small force based around four corvettes, a number of patrol craft, and land-based ocean surveillance radars. The navy is bolstered by the Finnish Border Guard, a paramilitary force that, while under the peacetime purview of the Ministry of the Interior, would evolve into a military force in a crisis.[85] In many ways, the Finnish security apparatus is well designed to respond to coercive and asymmetric actions, a result of Finland's historical experience. Finland's surface forces are augmented by two, relatively austere MPA operated by the Finnish Border Guard. This paucity of capabilities for MDA can be explained, in part, by Finland's overarching naval strategy. In a crisis, Finland would not use the maritime domain as a maneuver space but rather deny it to an adversary through advanced mines and land-based antiship cruise missiles.[86]

The Baltic states all have minimal capability for surface monitoring. Their navies contain small patrol craft that are only useful for monitoring territorial waters. There is no prospect for capability or capacity growth in this area due to the relatively high military priority each places on checking the challenge posed by Russia on land. The robust capability for aerial collection is the result of sustained NATO investment. Developing a system of mobile sea surveillance radars for the Baltic States may be advisable. However, it is unclear if the militaries of the Baltic states have the personnel to support this approach.

Subsurface

Germany's subsurface collection capability is based on eight P-3C MPA, six Type 212 submarines, and Lynx ASW helicopters.[87] These helicopters are scheduled to be replaced in the coming years by the ASW variant of the NH90. In addition, the P-3Cs are slated to have a complete overhaul of

---

[81] "Visby Class Corvette: Defining Stealth at Sea," Saab Solutions, accessed March 26, 2018, https://saab.com/naval/submarines-and-warships/naval-surface-ships/visby-class-corvette/.

[82] IISS, *Military Balance 2017*, 163.

[83] Interviews with Swedish security experts.

[84] "Åland—A Special Piece of Finland," *Visit Finland,* accessed February 7, 2018, http://www.visitfinland.com/article/aland-a-special-piece-of-finland/.

[85] Interviews with Finnish security experts.

[86] Interviews with Finnish security experts.

[87] IISS, *Military Balance 2017*, 117–18.

their mission systems, which should continue their relevance for the coming years.[88] The Type 212s have excellent shallow water capabilities in addition to air-independent propulsion (AIP) systems that allow them to remain submerged for extended periods, attributes well suited to the operational environment in the Baltic Sea.[89] In addition, the German Navy maintains substantial counter-mine capabilities including large counter-mine unmanned surface vessels (USVs) and dedicated minehunters.[90] However, this impressive set of capabilities belies deeper issues. The German P-3Cs were acquired secondhand from the Netherlands, the entire submarine fleet is down for maintenance, and its next-generation frigate program has no appreciable ASW capability and has been mired in controversy.[91] It is clear that Germany needs to increase its resource levels in the maritime domain to meet its ambitions.

Poland's capability for subsurface collection faces similar issues to its surface collection. Its capabilities are aging, comprised of one *Kilo*-class and four *Sokol*-class coast submarines.[92] The capability of the *Sokol*-class vessels is particularly suspect. At one point, Poland maintained a system of acoustic sensors in the Bay of Gdansk. The current state of this system is unknown; if operable, it is believed to be largely obsolete.[93] In contrast to surface assets, submarine acquisition does appear to be a priority for the Polish government.[94] This makes sense given the likely threat environment in the Baltic Sea; submarines represent a considerably more survivable investment in naval power. While this may close some gaps, Poland needs to develop capabilities and procedures to mitigate the threat posed by amphibious special forces and combat swimmers in the Bay of Gdansk.

Denmark's capabilities in this area have declined dramatically since the end of the Cold War. The Danish Navy completely divested its submarine force in the 2000s. The Danish Navy operates ASW helicopters and is in the process of acquiring the MH-60R Seahawk to replace its aging fleet of Lynx aircraft.[95] While these are excellent ASW helicopters, they cannot, by themselves, monitor the undersea domain. Its primary frigate class, the *Iver Huitfeldt*, lacks a towed sonar array.[96] The Danish Navy maintains a modular counter-mine capability for deployment on its surface vessels. This approach makes sense given the small size of the Danish Navy but is not as effective as a dedicated counter-mine force.

[88] Lockheed Martin, "Lockheed Martin Awarded $158.5 Million Upgrade Contract for Germany P-3C Orion Aircraft," *PR Newswire*, November 1, 2017, https://www.prnewswire.com/news-releases/lockheed-martin-awarded-1585-million-upgrade-contract-for-germany-p-3c-orion-aircraft-300546872.html.

[89] H. I. Sutton, "World Survey of AIP Submarines," *Convert Shores* (blog), March 19, 2016, http://www.hisutton.com/World%20survey%20of%20AIP%20submarines.html; and Alex Pape and Lee Willett, "Unseen but on the scene: German submarine technology delivers enhanced effect," *Janes International Defense Review*, 2017, http://www.janes.com/images/assets/331/72331/Unseen_but_on_scene_German_submarine_technology_delivers_enhanced_effect.pdf.

[90] IISS, *Military Balance 2017*, 117–18.

[91] Tyler Rogoway, "The German Navy Decided to Return Their Bloated New Frigate to the Ship Store This Christmas," *The War Zone,* December 23, 2017, http://www.thedrive.com/the-war-zone/17185/the-german-navy-has-decided-to-return-their-new-frigate-to-the-ship-store-this-christmas.

[92] Saunders, *Jane's Fighting Ships 2016–2017*, 645–46.

[93] Interviews with Polish security experts.

[94] "Three Bidders in Play for Poland's Orka Submarine Program," *Naval Today*, January 4, 2018, https://navaltoday.com/2018/01/04/three-bidders-in-play-for-polands-orka-submarine-program.

[95] Srijanee Chakraborthy, "Danish Navy Officially Takes Delivery of MH-60R Seahawk Helicopters from US Navy," *Naval Technology*, June 19, 2016, https://www.naval-technology.com/uncategorised/newsdanish-navy-officially-takes-delivery-of-mh-60r-seahawk-helicopters-from-us-navy-4926818.

[96] Saunders, *Jane's Fighting Ships 2016–2017*, 200.

Sweden has considerable capability for undersea detection given its advanced submarine force, led by its three SSK *Gotland*-class submarines, with the Sterling AIP-enabled endurance well suited for littoral environments like the Baltic Sea.[97] However, the recent incidents of potential Russian submarine intrusions highlight the difficulty in subsurface monitoring. This difficulty is increased by Sweden's complex littoral geography. The Swedish Navy's surface forces and aerial assets are less capable in undersea detection. Sweden's capability in this domain has atrophied considerably since the Cold War. The vital skills for undersea operations are far less common within the Swedish Navy today than they once were. Sweden is procuring two A26 submarines to replace the two aging *Sodermanland*-class vessels.[98] These advanced submarines may be further augmented by unmanned underwater vehicles (UUVs) to create additional capacity and unique shallow-water capabilities.

Finland is exceptionally proficient at mine warfare in both its offensive and defensive variants. The Finnish use of mines is a key aspect of its overall maritime strategy. Finland is also believed to maintain a system of acoustic sensors in the Gulf of Finland. The potential existence of this system was suggested by Finland's detection and prosecution of a submerged target, believed to be a foreign submarine in the waters off Helsinki, in 2015.[99] Beyond its territorial waters, Finland does not have a pronounced capability for subsurface collection. However, the capabilities it does possess are likely sufficient for the missions of the Finnish Armed Forces.

The Baltic states do not have considerable capabilities in this domain beyond counter-mine missions, primarily in their territorial waters. However, these mine warfare capabilities are noteworthy especially given the small sizes of their respective navies. In many ways, counter-mine missions are the primary focus of these navies. Latvia's counter-mine forces are particularly capable with NATO's Standing Mine Counter Measures Group One (SNMCGMG1) currently led by a Latvian commander.[100] However, the Baltic states face some of the same threats as Poland. Their proximity to Russian military installations in Kaliningrad and St. Petersburg creates vulnerabilities. They require the same capabilities for defending against small signature maritime forces as Poland.

Analysis

Effective analysis for MDA requires data integration and data analysis. Data integration focuses on the technical aspects of moving data from the point of collection to a central location and then the integration of heterogeneous data strains into a common system. Data analysis focuses on turning this data into information by both human analysts and automated processing. Considerable value is created in this process as patterns can be identified, behaviors catalogued, and greater insights derived. There are considerable issues facing both data integration and data analysis particularly in the Baltic Sea region. At present, these gaps result in fragmentation across the region in

---

[97] IISS, *Military Balance 2017*, 162; Pär Dahlander et al., "Smart Non-Nuclear Submarines in Changing Times: A HDW Group Industrial View," NATO/PFP UNCLASSIFIED (Norfolk, VA: NATO, 2002); and "SSK Gotland Class (Type A19)," *Naval Technology* (blog), accessed March 27, 2018, https://www.naval-technology.com/projects/gotland/.
[98] H. I. Sutton, "World Survey of AIP Submarines."
[99] "Finland Drops Depth Charges in 'Submarine' Alert," BBC News, April 28, 2015, http://www.bbc.com/news/world-europe-32498790.
[100] "Latvia Takes Command of Standing NATO Mine Counter Measures Group One for the First Time Ever," SARGS.LV, June 27, 2017, http://www.sargs.lv/Zinas/Military_News/2017/06/27-01.aspx.

confronting the Russia challenge. This section briefly highlights the existing architectures for both data integration and analysis and characterizes their shortcomings.

On the data integration front, the NATO states in the region have a solid foundation upon which to build. NATO standard datalinks, such as Link 16, provide a useful conduit for MDA data, especially that collected by military sensors. In addition, existing frameworks for the air domain to include the NATO Integrated Air and Missile Defense System (NATINADS) and the BALTNET framework provide key data integration for aerial sensors.[101] However, the NATO architecture is domain specific. It does not conceptualize the maritime domain in a holistic manner. Furthermore, the littoral nature of the Baltic Sea (and, to a lesser extent, the Norwegian Sea) means that a data integration system has to combine a very wide range of sensor inputs. Currently, such a system does not exist.

The biggest challenge from a technical perspective is the simple fact that Sweden and Finland, vital partner nations, are outside of NATO. From a perspective of datalinks and cryptography, this creates additional hurdles for achieving data integration of a sensitive/classified nature. To meet most of the challenges previously discussed, the integration of such data is a prerequisite.

There are systems and frameworks in place that attempt to bridge the Northern European seam. One such project is the European Defense Agency's Maritime Surveillance effort (MARSUR). This EU project aims to build a recognized maritime picture through the exchange of "operational maritime information."[102] While this project has reached an operational capability, it has not yet expanded to the point of sharing privileged information. Moreover, automatic data integration is still an objective, rather than achieved, capability.

In the Baltic Sea region, there are two additional frameworks worth noting. The first is SUCBAS, Sea Surveillance Co-Operation Baltic Sea, a cooperation agreement that includes Finland, Sweden, Denmark, Germany, Estonia, Latvia, Lithuania, Poland, and the United Kingdom. This expansive network has made good progress at facilitating data exchange in pursuit of a common operating picture. SUCBAS is designed to mitigate the issues resulting from organization mismatch when acting in a multinational manner. Much like MARSUR, SUCBAS seeks to achieve automated data sharing across these countries. However, SUCBAS Level III goes further with provisions for sharing classified data.[103] This is an important goal as it opens the door for sharing classified intelligence assessments built on MDA data. That said, SUCBAS Level III is yet to be implemented. While SUCBAS is a relatively large framework, the second framework of note, SUCFIS, Sea Surveillance Co-Operation Finland-Sweden, is bilateral. It functions in the same way as SUCBAS, and importantly, it presently enables classified data integration between the two nations.[104] This is in keeping with the deep cooperation between Finland and Sweden as shown by their bilateral standing naval task group.

---

[101] Republic of Latvia, "Cooperation of Air Forces," Ministry of Defence, accessed February 7, 2018, http://www.mod.gov.lv/en/Par_aizsardzibas_nozari/Politikas_istenosana/Baltijas_valstu_milit_sadarbiba/Gaisa.aspx; and NATO, "NATO Integrated Air and Missile Defence," February 9, 2016, https://www.nato.int/cps/ua/natohq /topics_8206.htm.
[102] European Defense Agency, "Maritime Surveillance (MARSUR)," June 1, 2017, https://www.eda.europa.eu/what-we-do/activities/activities-search/maritime-surveillance-(marsur).
[103] Sea Surveillance Co-Operation Baltic Sea (SUCBAS), "Levels," accessed February 7, 2018, http://sucbas.org/levels.
[104] Edward Lundquist, "Baltic Maritime Security," *Maritime Journal*, May 17, 2016, http://www.maritimejournal.com /news101/security-and-alarm-systems/baltic-maritime-security.

Analysis is the process by which additional insights are gleaned from the collected data. The frameworks and cooperation agreements described above provide for data integration but no data analysis, the second requisite element for effective MDA. The individual nations of the Baltic Sea region do not have the ability to fully analyze the operational environments in an independent manner. Most states in the region lack the military capacity to sustain a dedicated career field in maritime intelligence. For officers that do develop this specialty, it is often part of a wider set of responsibilities, and there is a lack of institutional support for these skills over the course of a career. These issues will only be exacerbated as data collection increases thanks to the adoption of advanced capabilities like the F-35 Joint Strike Fighter and, potentially, integration of unmanned systems in European force structures.[105] Maintaining a maritime or littoral analytic organization is also relatively expensive, especially given the need to consistently staff such an organization in peacetime. It is not a capability that can be kept in reserve and activated in a period of crisis.

Germany is building a Baltic Maritime Component Command (BMCC) at Rostock. This organization is a German national initiative with an eye toward multinational operations. It is slated to consist of approximately 100 German staff with additional billets for 25 multinational officers.[106] From the perspective of data analysis, the BMCC could serve as a data fusion center for the Baltic Sea region. In this way, it could help to close the seam between Northern European partners and NATO. This fusion center could be used to support deep analysis into maritime hybrid issues and build a broader understanding of likely Russian actions and deployment patterns. A dedicated analytic center could also offer support for a multinational cadre of intelligence officers throughout their careers. A multinational approach to the problem of MDA analysis in the Baltic Sea is the path forward given the relatively small size of regional navies. On their own, they lack the capacity to support such functions, but if integrated, they could comfortably maintain a pooled analytic capability.

Action

Once collected and analyzed, information must be able to move to needed platforms and consumers for MDA to be effective. This function covers two areas: resiliency and operational frameworks. Resiliency is the ability to continue to transmit data and information in the face of adversary jamming and other nonkinetic attacks. Operational frameworks are existing structures that knit together multinational capabilities into a cohesive whole. The countries in the Baltic Sea region are not resilient in the face of existing threats and lack the structures to combine their capabilities in a meaningful way.

With regards to resiliency, it is not an overreaction to question the reliability of all forms of wireless communication technology in a crisis scenario. The latest generation of electronic warfare capabilities is likely highly effective against most, if not all, NATO standard datalinks. This problem only worsens when considering the potentially less sophisticated and secure datalinks currently used by other actors in the maritime domain. Mitigating this threat will require new technological approaches to both reduce the overall data transmission requirements and increase the overall resiliency to advanced jamming. Doctrinal changes are also required to enable personnel and

---

[105] Interviews with Baltic security experts.
[106] Magnus Nordenman, "Back to the North," Atlantic Council, April 2017, 4, http://www.atlanticcouncil.org /images/publications/Back_to_the_North_web_0406.pdf.

platforms that can effectively operate and create domain awareness, albeit in a more limited fashion, in the face of such threats.

The lack of operational frameworks is somewhat surprising given the prevalence of NATO nations in the region. While the alliance has a robust array of command structures for maritime operations, they are not well suited to the Baltic Sea environment. There are a number of bilateral agreements throughout the region that knit together specific nations. These agreements include those between Finland and Estonia, Finland and Sweden, the United States and Finland, and a deepening relationship between Germany and Sweden. The Finnish-Swedish relationship is the closest in the region with the two nations operating a combined maritime task force.

The United States has also worked to create some level of operational cooperation in the region through the annual BALTOPS exercise. While this is a laudable effort, it does not achieve an increase in operational coordination and cooperation over the long term. The issue with BALTOPS is that it creates operational requirements built around the exercise rather than steady-state missions. In addition, it can promote a cargo cult mentality among some participants who come to rely on U.S. capabilities.

Beyond BALTOPS, the United States has shown limited willingness to lead on Baltic Sea security. Sustained political commitment from the region's nations is a prerequisite for delivering the level of day-to-day operational capability and cooperation needed to succeed against the Russian challenge set. The German-led BMCC could serve as the focal point for a Baltic Sea region operational framework. However, there are considerable political hurdles for both Germany and some of its neighbors to overcome to fulfill this role. Of importance, the BMCC would need to be an operational organization capable of linking collection, analysis, and action in contingencies. Contributing nations would have to commit to provide the necessary assets. If it proves instead to be merely a coordinating body of liaison officers from around the region, another regional framework for the MDA operational challenge should be sought.

Norwegian Sea

The most salient challenge to maritime domain awareness in the Norwegian Sea region is the increasing difficulty of detecting advanced submarines. NATO and its key partners are generally ill-prepared for acoustic detection of Russia's latest generation of submarines. Although the alliance has undertaken some mitigating steps, there is a pressing need to match technological investments with personnel resources. Also problematic is the need to unify ASW and missile defense operations and increase the analytic capacity for understanding evolving patterns of behavior in the region's maritime domain. The threats from long-range strike weapons discussed earlier in this study are also more evident in the Norwegian Sea than in the Baltic Sea.

Collection

The maritime domain capabilities NATO fields in the Norwegian Sea region are relatively strong. Aerial and surface collection are generally adequate, with collection in support of cruise missile defense a remaining area of concern. However, NATO and its partners lack the local capacity to support the continuous deployment of assets needed to support steady-state MDA activities and rely heavily on globally tasked U.S. forces. Subsurface targets present the most significant collection challenge. Existing technologies and operational paradigms are insufficient to meet the challenge posed by the latest generation of Russian submarines.

Aerial

The *United States* has robust capabilities to support aerial collection in the region, including both Europe-based and other forces. In Europe, the United States bases four Aegis destroyers in Rota, Spain.[107] Although these destroyers are generally tasked in support of U.S. and NATO ballistic missile defense missions, they could be deployed to the North or Norwegian Seas in a crisis. The United States and Norway also jointly operate a radar facility on the island of Vardo. While the exact capabilities of this radar are classified, it is widely believed to be used for missile defense and technical intelligence missions.[108] The United States has not routinely deployed E-3 Sentry AWACS aircraft to the region, but it did include an E-3 in the 2017 BALTOPS exercise. These aircraft could operate in support of Northern European missions from a variety of U.S. and allied bases throughout Europe.[109] Should the U.S. Navy have a carrier battle group in the region, it would dramatically increase U.S. capabilities for aerial collection. Not only would this add numerous Aegis vessels, it would include the additional AEW aircraft.

The *United Kingdom* similarly has considerable aerial detection capabilities for this region. The most notable set of systems is the chain of radar stations around the edges of the British Isles. These radars are the descendants of the famed Chain Home radars of World War II. For the purpose of monitoring Norwegian Sea airspace, the radar site at Saxa Vord at the northern tip of the Shetland Islands is key. While this radar facility was closed in 2006, the Royal Air Force is currently reopening the facility.[110] This is bolstered by six E-3D Sentry AWACS aircraft and an exceptionally capable air defense destroyer, the Type 45.[111] UK capabilities will likely grow in the coming years as the Royal Navy begins to build a carrier battle group around the newly commissioned HMS *Queen Elizabeth*. However, like the United States, the United Kingdom faces an ongoing mission-capacity gap. The British armed forces have been considerably reduced since 2011, which at times can leave the British "back yard" under-watched.

Norway operates an array of ground-based radars under the SINDRE system and is currently working on upgrading key elements of these radars.[112] These fixed radars are inherently more survivable than the fixed systems in the Baltic Sea region as they are mounted in a fortified and retractable installation. The Royal Norwegian Navy also maintains a significant air surveillance

[107] U.S. Naval Forces Europe-Africa, "USS Carney Joins Other FDNF Ships in Rota, Spain," September 25, 2015, http://www.navy.mil/submit/display.asp?story_id=91243.

[108] Thomas Nilsen, "U.S. Spends $50 million on Vardo radar upgrade," *The Barents Observer*, February 27, 2013, http://barentsobserver.com/en/security/2013/02/us-spends-50-million-vardo-radar-upgrade-27-02.

[109] Caleb Wanzer, "Air Force Brings E-3 Sentry to NATO Exercise for First Time in 20 Years," U.S. Department of Defense, June 2, 2017, https://www.defense.gov/News/Article/Article/1201281/air-force-brings-e-3-sentry-to-nato-exercise-for-first-time-in-20-years.

[110] "New Saxa Vord Radar Nears Completion," *Shetland News*, January 27, 2018, http://www.shetnews.co.uk/news/15805-new-saxa-vord-radar-nears-completion; and Chris Cope, "Unst Radar Base Work to Begin in October," *Shetland News*, September 16, 2017, http://www.shetnews.co.uk/newsbites/15195-unst-radar-base-work-to-begin-in-october.

[111] Saunders, *Jane's Fighting Ships 2016–2017*, 896.

[112] Umesh Ellichipuram, "Saab to Upgrade SINDRE I Air Surveillance Radars in Norway," *Air Force Technology*, October 13, 2017, http://www.airforce-technology.com/news/newssaab-to-upgrade-sindre-i-air-surveillance-radars-in-norway-5948440.

capability in its five *Fridtjof Nansen*-class frigates. These relatively small vessels mount a full version of the Aegis combat system. Norway's greatest capability challenge in the Norwegian Sea is its failure to keep pace with rapidly evolving Russian forces operating an expanded long-range strike complex. Norway also suffers from a considerable readiness issue. Although it owns five frigates and is slated to increase its crews accordingly in the coming years, Norway today only has crews for three frigates.[113] Reaching its five-crew goal should dramatically increase the availability of its frigate fleet.

Canada's armed forces are unlikely to provide much assistance with air surveillance activities in the Norwegian Sea. The Royal Canadian Navy is currently considering how to best replace its surface fleet. Its current fleet lags considerably behind its European counterparts; it would be a minor contributor to a NATO naval formation in the region. The *Halifax*-class frigates have recently received upgrades to their radar and combat weapons systems, which will improve their capabilities.[114] However, they should not be confused for purpose-built air warfare frigates. Canada is at the early stages of a comprehensive modernization of its Navy and Coast Guard under the National Shipbuilding Procurement Strategy. The surface warship component, the Single Class Surface Combatant Project, will result in a dramatic increase in capability for the Royal Canadian Navy.[115]

The *Netherlands* has excellent naval capabilities albeit small capacity. The Dutch operate four of the *De Zeven Provincien*-class air defense frigates. These vessels mount a similar combat weapon system as the German F124 *Sachsen*-class frigates.[116] These vessels can integrate into NATO's BMD architecture and have demonstrated this role at several exercises.[117] While these are very capable vessels, their small number raises capacity concerns for steady-state air surveillance missions. Dutch ground-based capabilities are unlikely to contribute meaningfully to aerial surveillance of the Norwegian Sea.

NATO can provide considerable air surveillance capabilities through the 16 E-3C Sentries in the alliance's shared capability set.[118] These aircraft are based out of Geilenkrichen, Germany. However, these assets are in exceptionally high demand and would be under considerable tasking stress in a contingency scenario. These aircraft are also aging and the alliance is considering how to best replace them, a process likely to last until the mid- to late 2020s.[119] Furthermore, there are concerns about the survivability of all AWACS (and similar) aircraft against exceptionally long-range

[113] Stelios Kanavkis, "Analysis: The Norwegian Navy Under the 2017–2020 Long Term Defence Plan," *Navy Recognition*, June 30, 2016, http://www.navyrecognition.com/index.php/focus-analysis/naval-technology/4153-analysis-the-norwegian-navy-under-the-2017-2020-long-term-defence-plan.html.

[114] "Modernizing Canada's Halifax Class Frigates," *Defense Industry Daily*, February 1, 2018, https://www.defenseindustrydaily.com/modernizing-canadas-halifax-class-frigates-05062.

[115] David Pugliese, "Canada's Massive Surface-Combatant Program to Get Underway This Summer," *Defense News*, July 27, 2016, https://www.defensenews.com/home/2016/07/27/canada-s-massive-surface-combatant-program-to-get-underway-this-summer.

[116] Saunders, *Jane's Fighting Ships 2016–2017*, 570.

[117] U.S. Naval Forces Europe-Africa / U.S. 6th Fleet, "Formidable Shield 2017: Ship Engages BMD Target During NATO Exercise, MDA and Navy Conduct SM-6 Test Launch," October 15, 2017, http://www.c6f.navy.mil/news/formidable-shield-2017-ship-engages-bmd-target-during-nato-exercise-mda-and-navy-conduct-sm-6.

[118] NATO, "AWACS: NATO's 'Eyes in the Sky,'" September 28, 2017, https://www.nato.int/cps/en/natolive/topics_48904.htm.

[119] Gareth Jennings, "NATO Begins Study of AWACS Replacement," *Jane's 360*, February 17, 2017, http://www.janes.com/article/67813/nato-begins-study-of-awacs-replacement.

surface-to-air and air-to-air weapons explicitly designed to target these platforms. Lastly, it is unclear the extent to which these aircraft can support the anti-cruise missile component of the air defense mission. An aerial layer sensor that can look "down" on low flying missiles is a key element in defeating these weapons.

Surface

The *United States* maintains considerable technical means for space-based tracking of surface vessels. While these capabilities are classified, it is believed that the United States operates both imagery and electronic collection platforms that can track individual vessels. These exquisite capabilities are combined with significant surface and aerial systems. The U.S. Navy has resumed rotational deployments of P-3C to Keflavik in Iceland and plans to deploy the newer P-8 MPA once base infrastructure has been upgraded.[120] While the deployment of these aircraft is largely driven by the subsurface threat, they have considerable ability to track surface vessels. They are likely supported by deployed U.S. submarines and surface vessels operating near the Norwegian Sea. As noted previously, submarines (and acoustic tracking more broadly) can help to build an understanding of adversary pattern of life by matching vessels to their unique acoustic signatures. While the United States has considerable capabilities in this domain, its MPA force is no longer adequately postured to operate in the Norwegian Sea region on a steady-state basis. Furthermore, the U.S. Navy has global commitments and is "rebalanced" for threats emanating from the Pacific region. This reality means that new, advanced systems that could improve surface collection, such as the MQ-4C Triton unmanned aircraft, will first be deployed to the Pacific, rather than European, theater.

The *United Kingdom* has a concerning lack of capability in this space. At present, the British armed forces do not operate any maritime patrol aircraft having retired the Nimrod MR2 in 2010.[121] The 2015 Strategic Defence and Security Review (SDSR) committed to reacquiring this capability in the form of nine P-8 Poseidon aircraft.[122] In the interim, British aircrews have been maintaining their proficiency in this mission set by embedding personnel within units from Australia, Canada, New Zealand, and the United States.[123] With regards to surface units, the Royal Navy operates 13 Type 23 frigates in addition to the 6 Type 45 destroyers mentioned previously. These vessels have considerable surface surveillance capabilities and embark multirole helicopters.[124] Note that while the United Kingdom maintains both a Border Force and Coastguard, many roles often handled by coast guards, such as exclusive economic zone (EEZ) enforcement, are conducted by the Royal Navy. The capacity issues plaguing the British armed forces are apparent here as well. The general-purpose Type 23s are aging with ongoing concerns about their reliability and maintenance requirements. They are scheduled to be replaced starting in the early to mid-2020s by the larger

---

[120] Steven Beardsley, "Navy Aircraft Returning to Former Cold War Base in Iceland," *Stars and Stripes*, February 9, 2016, https://www.stripes.com/news/navy-aircraft-returning-to-former-cold-war-base-in-iceland-1.393156.
[121] "Nimrod Officially Retires after Three Decades," *The Telegraph*, March 26, 2010, http://www.telegraph.co.uk/news /uknews/defence/7528840/Nimrod-officially-retires-after-three-decades.html.
[122] Ministry of Defence, *National Security Strategy and Strategic Defence and Security Review 2015* (London, UK, 2015), 28, https://www.gov.uk/government/uploads/system/uploads/attachment_data/file/555607 /2015_Strategic_Defence_and_Security_Review.pdf.
[123] Ministry of Defense, Office of the Secretary of State for Scotland, "Defence Secretary Announces New Maritime Patrol Aircraft Squadrons," *GOV.UK*, July 13, 2017, https://www.gov.uk/government/news/defence-secretary-announces-new-maritime-patrol-aircraft-squadrons.
[124] Saunders, *Jane's Fighting Ships 2016–2017*, 896–98.

Type 26 and the more austere Type 31.[125] Until these new MPA and surface vessels enter service, there are likely to be worsening capacity gaps. The Type 23 fleet is operating well beyond its intended lifespan. Some reports indicate that the United Kingdom may divest a sizable portion of its frigate fleet before replacements reach the fleet.[126]

Norway currently operates six P-3C MPA in addition to the five multirole frigates discussed previously.[127] These provide an adequate capability for surface surveillance. Furthermore, the *Fridtjof Nansen*-class vessels can embark the naval variant of the NH90 helicopter, which further improves their surface collection capabilities. However, these helicopters have been long delayed and Norway is considering canceling the tender and searching for an alternative.[128] In addition to these large surface vessels, the Royal Norwegian Navy also operates six of the unique *Skjold*-class corvettes for littoral operations.[129] These vessels are capable of extreme speeds utilizing surface effects. The overall Norwegian capability for surface surveillance is sufficient but concerns remain about the overall capacity and readiness levels, especially for steady-state activities.

Canada's capability for surface collection is considerably greater than its capabilities in the aerial domain. The six *Halifax*-class frigates based in Halifax, Nova Scotia, provide ample capability and can each carry a single helicopter to improve their surface surveillance abilities.[130] These surface vessels represent the primary deployable elements of the Royal Canadian Navy (RCN) with smaller vessels and Canada's excellent coast guard focusing on issues closer to home. The RCN also operates 16 CP-140 Aurora MPA, based on the P-3 Orion airframe. The surface surveillance capabilities of these aircraft have dramatically improved in recent years, due to upgrades primarily designed to support the employment of these aircraft in overland surveillance missions.[131] Looking to the future, the RCN is procuring five Harry *DeWolf*-class offshore patrol vessels (OPVs). These are very large, ice-capable OPVs optimized for operations in the Arctic and could prove useful for NATO operations in the high north.[132] The aforementioned Single Class Surface Combatant will likely represent an improvement over the *Halifax*-class for this mission. The primary challenge to the RCN's surface collection capability is the aging of its platforms, which drives up maintenance costs and limits operational availability.

The *Netherlands* has dramatically less surface surveillance capability now than it did at the beginning of the 2000s. The primary reason for this decrease is the divestment of the entire Dutch fleet of 13 P-3C MPA in the early 2000s without replacement.[133] The Royal Netherlands Navy does maintain a small surface fleet of relatively advanced vessels. Beyond the previously mentioned air defense frigates, they operate four OPVs. These vessels, while excellent, are often called on for

125 Andrew Chuter, "UK Deadline for Type 31 Frigates 'Just Not Going to Happen,'" *Defense News*, August 25, 2017, https://www.defensenews.com/naval/2017/08/25/uk-deadline-for-type-31-frigates-just-not-going-to-happen.
126 Deborah Haynes, "Britain Mulls Warships Sale as Military Cuts Deepen," *The Times*, October 26, 2017, https://www.thetimes.co.uk/edition/news/britain-mulls-warships-sale-as-military-cuts-deepen-2j0d0s5bs.
127 IISS, *Military Balance 2017*, 143.
128 Thorstein Korsvold, "NH90: Forsvaret vurderer alternative løsninger," *AldriMer.No*, October 27, 2017, https://www.aldrimer.no/nh90-forsvaret-vurderer-alternative-losninger/.
129 Saunders, *IHS Jane's Fighting Ships 2016–2017*, 594.
130 Ibid., 104.
131 Col. Iain Huddleston, "Changing with the Times: The Evolution of Canada's CP-140 Aurora," *Canadian Naval Review* 11, number 1 (Spring 2015), http://www.navalreview.ca/wp-content/uploads/public/vol11num1/vol11num1art2.pdf.
132 Saunders, *IHS Jane's Fighting Ships 2016–2017*, 107.
133 Hicks et al., *Undersea Warfare in Northern Europe*.

coast guard missions in the Caribbean.[134] The Dutch also operate 12 NH90 that can further support surface surveillance.[135] The lack of a long-range, fixed-wing MPA substantially impairs the Dutch ability to monitor large areas such as the North or Norwegian Seas.

NATO does not maintain a pooled capability for surface maritime surveillance. Alliance Ground Surveillance (AGS) is a pooled acquisition of five RQ-4B Global Hawk Block 40 based out of NATO Base Sigonella in Sicily.[136] While this is a system designed for ground surveillance, its advanced radar could be used in a maritime setting. However, the operational demands on the AGS are great; it is unlikely it would be tasked against Northern European collection requirements.

Subsurface

There is a universal issue facing all of these nations with regards to subsurface collection. They all have dramatically depleted stockpiles of sonobuoys and may not have the budgets necessary to support the robust employment of these disposable sensors in steady-state monitoring of the undersea domain. Acquiring sufficient sonobuoys is vital but will also likely become more challenging in the years ahead. Advances in submarine quieting will necessitate more advanced and more expensive sonobuoys.

The *United States* operates the world's preeminent submarine force as well as a range of supporting capabilities including the MH-60R ASW helicopter, P-8 Poseidon and P-3C Orion MPA, and specialized sonar ships equipped with exceptionally sensitive acoustic sensors. This impressive array of systems belies some deeper issues with U.S. collection efforts in the subsurface domain. Most of the U.S. Navy's surface and aviation assets have been only tertiarily focused on undersea warfare readiness over the past two decades. The need to support ongoing combat operations in the Middle East has led to a decline in the skills necessary to conduct these missions. Moreover, the U.S. Navy no longer has the capacity it once did for ASW. This is most evident in the lack of a U.S. frigate class optimized for ASW operations. These trends have been worsened by global advances in submarine quieting that dramatically increase the difficulty in detecting and tracking adversary vessels. It is unclear if the existing array of surface and aviation assets are effective in operations targeting the latest generation of ultra-quiet Russian submarines. Furthermore, the U.S. submarine force is ill-suited to operations in tight, shallow littoral environments given the large size of U.S. vessels.

The *United Kingdom* operates a submarine force smaller than that of the United States but approaching its quality in technical merit and personnel skill. The Royal Navy plans to procure seven of the excellent *Astute*-class SSNs by the mid-2020s.[137] However, the British have experienced cost growth and construction delays on these vessels. The Royal Navy's surface force, notably the Type 23 frigates, are excellent in ASW operations mounting an advanced variable-depth sonar system.[138] The replacement Type 26 frigates will be similarly equipped. As with their

---

[134] "Dutch OPV HNLMS Zeeland wraps up four-month Caribbean stint," *Naval Today,* November 10, 2017, https://navaltoday.com/2017/11/10/dutch-opv-hnlms-zeeland-wraps-up-four-month-caribbean-stint/.
[135] IISS, *Military Balance 2017,* 140.
[136] Public Diplomacy Division, "Alliance Ground Surveillance (AGS) Factsheet," NATO, July 2016, https://www.nato.int /nato_static_fl2014/assets/pdf/pdf_2016_07/20160627_1607-factsheet-ags-en.pdf.
[137] Saunders, *IHS Jane's Fighting Ships 2016–2017,* 894.
[138] Ibid., 898.

submarines, this is not a wholly good news story, with budgetary issues curtailing the Royal Navy's overall capacity. Finally, the United Kingdom is without an MPA force for the next several years. This key gap has been dramatically highlighted by purported Russian submarine activity near Faslane. The British had to request NATO MPA support to monitor the waters near their most sensitive naval facility.[139]

Norway operates a small submarine force of six *Ula*-class SSKs.[140] While these vessels have been upgraded over the years, they are slated to be replaced by four variants of the German Type 212 SSP.[141] This will dramatically improve the capability of the Royal Norwegian Navy's submarine fleet and likely allow it to contribute more substantially to undersea warfare operations in the Norwegian Sea. The submarine force is augmented by the aforementioned P-3C Orion aircraft. The six P-3C Orion aircraft will be replaced by five P-8 Poseidon MPA between 2022 and 2023.[142] The effect of this small number of platforms is dramatically boosted by geography: they are based at Andoya on the northeastern edge of the Norwegian Sea. The *Fridtjof Nansen*-class vessels can also contribute to subsurface collection by embarking a single ASW helicopter and deploying their towed array sonars. Overall, Norway retains a solid core of capabilities in this domain and its planned acquisitions should maintain its position. There are questions about the efficacy of smaller, nonnuclear submarines in open-ocean search missions against the very latest nuclear-powered vessels. An approach that integrates a range of platforms is likely the solution; however, this raises questions about the effective networking of aerial, surface, and subsurface assets.

Canada's capabilities for undersea collection are uneven. Canada's MPA fleet has been substantially upgraded to improve acoustic processing equipment and sonobuoys. These modifications mean that the CP-140 Auroras are some of the best sub-hunting aircraft in the world despite their aging airframes.[143] The RCN's submarine fleet, by comparison, is in a poor state. The four *Victoria*-class SSKs were acquired second hand from the United Kingdom in the early 2000s and are split between Canada's Pacific and Atlantic fleets.[144] They have been plagued with a series of reliability issues and accidents. In addition, the vessels themselves are old; they originally launched into British service as early as 1986.[145] For this reason, a recent report of the Canadian Standing Senate Committee on National Security and Defense called for the procurement of 12 modern submarines to meet Canada's future security needs.[146] The state of the Canadian surface fleet is somewhere between its MPAs and submarines. The *Halifax*-class, while aging, has significant capabilities for

[139] Ben Farmer, "Britain forced to ask Nato to track 'Russian submarine' in Scottish waters," *The Telegraph*, December 9, 2014, http://www.telegraph.co.uk/news/uknews/defence/11283926/Britain-forced-to-ask-Nato-to-track-Russian-submarine-in-Scottish-waters.html.

[140] IISS, *Military Balance 2017*, 143.

[141] Sebastian Schulte, "Norway opts to buy German submarines," *Janes 360*, February 8, 2017, http://www.janes.com/article/67555/norway-opts-to-buy-german-submarines.

[142] Aaron Mehta, "Pentagon seeks increased P-8 ties with Norway, UK," *Defense News*, July 3, 2017, https://www.defensenews.com/air/2017/07/03/pentagon-seeks-increased-p-8-ties-with-norway-uk/.

[143] Robin Laird, "Who Stands on Guard for Thee: Canada's Contribution to Northern Defense," *Breaking Defense*, August 15, 2017, https://breakingdefense.com/2017/08/who-stands-on-guard-for-thee-canadas-contribution-to-northern-defense/.

[144] Saunders, *IHS Jane's Fighting Ships 2016–2017*, 102.

[145] Ibid.

[146] "Reinvesting in the Canadian Armed Forces: A Plan for the Future," Report of the Standing Senate Committee on National Security and Defence, vii, May 2017, https://sencanada.ca/content/sen/committee/421/SECD/reports/SECDDPRReport_FINAL_e.pdf.

undersea collection with a towed sonar array that will only be further improved with the integration of the new CH-148 Cyclone ASW helicopter.[147]

The *Netherlands* operates a small force of four *Walrus*-class SSKs. These vessels are in the midst of a modernization and life-extension program that should see them serving until the mid-2020s. These upgrades are a stopgap measure until the Dutch can procure a new submarine class. This program is believed to commence around 2025.[148] The surface fleet has minimal capabilities for subsurface collection, mainly through embarked ASW helicopters. Given the divestment of MPA, there is no long-range undersea collection capability. While the Royal Netherlands Navy can credibly conduct subsurface collection in the North Sea, its capabilities in the wider North Atlantic, to include the Norwegian Sea, are minimal.

NATO does not operate any pooled capability for subsurface collection. Some have suggested a multinational or NATO procurement of an MPA.[149] While this is an approach to cover the gaps caused by the decline of NATO's combined capability for undersea collection, it has yet to move forward, and it is unclear how such a proposal would evolve.

Analysis

As previously discussed in the study team's assessment of analysis capabilities for the Baltic Sea, NATO has several domain-specific sharing agreements for air defense data. NATO Integrated Air and Missile Defense (NATINAMDS) includes the fixed radar sites that ring the Norwegian Sea and numerous NATO navies feed data into the NATO BMD architecture.[150] This structure can handle the data integration for air defense missions. A major issue for the Norwegian Sea is that the United States is often unwilling to share information about the undersea domain. The high classification surrounding U.S. information on the subsurface domain limits sharing to only one or two allies, if at all. This problem will continue to hamper an integrated MDA approach for the Norwegian Sea.

In addition, effective MDA in the Norwegian Sea will require the integration of data from undersea platforms. For fixed acoustic arrays, this is less of an issue as they can be hardwired to ashore facilities. For mobile arrays, submarines, and UUVs, this is a difficult challenge. Undersea data transmission is characterized by short ranges, low bandwidths, and high latencies. There are some technical approaches that can help to better integrate these undersea platforms into a holistic MDA framework. These include unmanned surface vehicles and seabed infrastructure acting as network gateways as well as disposable, single-use communications buoys. Data-integration issues are critically compounded by the lack of a data-integration framework or analysis center that is focused on understanding the Norwegian Sea on a day-to-day basis.

---

[147] "CH-148 CYCLONE," *Canadian Defense Review*, August 22, 2017, http://www.canadiandefencereview.com /Featured_content?blog/78.
[148] Saunders, *IHS Jane's Fighting Ships 2016–2017*, 568.
[149] NATO, "Pooling Maritime Patrol Aircraft," December 2012, https://www.nato.int/cps/en/natolive/news_93218.htm; and Magnus Nordenman, "NATO's Next Consortium: Maritime Patrol Aircraft," Atlantic Council, May 2016, http://www.atlanticcouncil.org/images/publications/NATOs_Next_Consortium_web_0506_1.pdf.
[150] NATO, "NATO Ballistic Missile Defence Architecture as of 2016: Protecting NATO's Populations, Territory, and Forces," July 11, 2016, https://www.nato.int/nato_static_fl2014/assets/pdf/pdf_2016_07/20160711_160709-bmd-def-architecture.pdf.

At present, this shortcoming is framed in the context of theater ASW, but as this study has argued, the threat is more complex than simply tracking adversary submarines in this region. Theater ASW can be thought of as the unification of collection, analysis, and action to address the submarine threat. In this way, it nests neatly under this study's MDA framework. During the Cold War, NATO oriented to this problem through Combined Task Force 84, tasked with the Atlantic ASW mission.[151] While this organization still exists, it does not have the ASW Operations Centers (ASWOCs) and assigned MPA forces that it once enjoyed.[152] The ASWOCs were a vital component in understanding the threat as they supported steady-state monitoring of vital areas. These centers also maintained a Consolidated Maritime Briefing Book, a confidential document used to disseminate key findings about Russian operational patters, share best practices for target prosecution, and deconflict allied submarine activity.

The last ASWOC was closed in 2002. Reportedly, the Consolidated Maritime Briefing Books that advanced shared learning have been lost to the alliance.[153] If true, this represents the near total forfeiture of NATO muscle memory for Atlantic ASW. CTF 84 still exists as one of the myriad responsibilities for the U.S. Commander Submarine Forces / Commander Submarine Force Atlantic (COMSUBFOR / COMSUBLANT). The unique role of COMSUBFOR within the U.S. Navy's structure includes both administrative and operational control over U.S. submarine and ASW forces.[154] This raises considerable questions as to how well resourced the traditional roles and responsibilities of CTF 84 are today. Put simply, NATO and the U.S. Navy are not adequately oriented to the analytic challenge of the subsurface domain across Northern European waters.

MARCOM, NATO's maritime component headquarters, is not resourced at a level to support steady-state, theater-level analysis of the Norwegian Sea.[155] National capabilities for this mission likely exist, especially within the U.S. Navy. However, the analytic experience and deep expertise required for traditional naval intelligence missions has decayed. Shortcomings in personnel focused on traditional maritime intelligence functions is a major gap for NATO to overcome, after years overwhelmingly focused on assessing intelligence in the land domain. Given the Cold War strength of NATO in maritime intelligence, the degree to which the alliance has lost its advantage should shock the West. It will be difficult to rebuild the capacity and capability quickly.[156]

Action

When considering NATO's capability for action in the Norwegian Sea, data resiliency is less of a concern than in the Baltic Sea region. Russia does not enjoy a geographic advantage in this region that would allow it to position powerful electronic warfare capabilities close to vital command and control and intelligence facilities. In addition, the tactical, line-of-sight datalinks that would support

---

[151] Cdr. William Perkins (USN), *Alliance Airborne Anti-Submarine Warfare: A Forecast for Maritime Air ASW in the Future Operational Environment* (Kalkar, Germany: Joint Air Power Competence Centre, June 2016), https://www.japcc.org/wp-content/uploads/JAPCC_ASW_web.pdf.

[152] Ibid., 17–19.

[153] Ibid., 19.

[154] Vice Adm. Joe Tofalo (USN), "Commander Submarine Forces Atlantic Command Brief," Slide 3-7, http://www.public.navy.mil/subfor/hq/Documents/COMSUBFORCOMSUBLANT%20Command%20Brief.pdf.

[155] Interviews with NATO security experts.

[156] Interviews with maritime intelligence experts.

NATO operations in this region are fairly robust and resistant to jamming. The resiliency of beyond-line-of-sight satellite communications is a greater concern.

NATO's operational frameworks for theater ASW and by extension steady-state MDA activities in the Norwegian Sea have atrophied dramatically over the past 20-plus years. The ASWOCs were a key component not only in analysis but also in coordinating responses. There no longer exists an interwoven command and control and intelligence fabric. Further, the absorption of the CTF 84 structure into COMSUBFOR's broader portfolio eliminated a dedicated operational commander and staff for these missions. MARCOM is also not presently structured to fulfill this mission. It does not control the schedules of the Standing NATO Maritime Groups (SNMGs), which could be tasked for steady-state missions. Rather, the schedules for SNMG engagements are controlled by Supreme Headquarters Allied Powers Europe (SHAPE). These command and control arrangements hamper the alliance's ability to rapidly shift the SNMGs in a contingency scenario without approval from the NATO Advisory Council (NAC), dramatically limiting their flexibility.[157]

NATO appears to be waking up to these challenges. Of note, the alliance recently released Experimental Tactics publication 197 (EXTAC), which proposes an area ASW commander.[158] The EXTAC 197 proposal in turn may be realized in the forthcoming establishment of an Atlantic Command (ACOM), likely following the July 2018 NATO summit. A reestablished ACOM could dramatically improve the NATO's focus and command and control arrangements for theater ASW operations.[159] Such a move by the allies would signal an acknowledgment of the need to revive successful Cold War-era frameworks for confronting the submarine threat in the North Atlantic. Given the changed nature of the Russian threat, a new ACOM would need to look forward even more than it looks back, conceptualizing the challenge set in the broadest possible terms. Although a positive step for the alliance, this new command may take nearly a decade to fully set up.[160] NATO and its partners cannot afford to stand still in the interim. The West will need to undertake steps now to improve its MDA capabilities and close identified operational gaps.

---

[157] Interviews with NATO security experts.
[158] Perkins, "Alliance Airborne Antisubmarine Warfare: A Forecast for Maritime Air ASW in the Future Operational Environment."
[159] Interviews with maritime intelligence experts.
[160] Interviews with maritime intelligence experts.

Chapter 4: Recommendations

NATO and its regional partners, Sweden and Finland, need to take a range of steps to better integrate MDA capabilities in the Baltic Sea and Norwegian Sea regions. The threats facing these nations combined with the nature of MDA necessitate a relatively seamless approach that works across national and alliance boundaries. Achieving this goal will not be without challenges and, in some instances, considerable difficulties given the character of regional relationships. Ultimately, effective MDA in these regions will require enhanced collection, improved analysis, and prompt action.

A Regional Approach: Guiding Strategy

Improving MDA capabilities across Northern Europe is a laudable goal. However, these investments will not be effective unless they are integrated into an overarching political and military strategy for countering Russian coercive and destabilizing actions. A core element of a strategy to achieve this goal is tailoring and modulating responses to achieve the desired effects without risking tit-for-tat escalation.

At the political level, the nations of the Baltic Sea region need to develop a common understanding of the Russia challenge and agree to a common set of political response options. This will in turn foster a discussion of how the military instrument can be used in pursuit of common goals. Given the scope and nature of the Russian threat, an effective regional MDA architecture, and constituent national capabilities, will be required for any conceivable political-military goals. This capability cannot stop at the water's edge. Instead, Baltic Sea MDA must be truly littoral given the tyranny of the region's compressed geography.

In the Norwegian Sea region, the requisite political cohesion is well-established. The vital troika of Norway, the United Kingdom, and the United States is committed to confronting renewed Russian activity, including undersea. These nations now should work to deepen their cooperation, incorporate other NATO states and NATO partners with relevant capabilities, and create an integrated MDA capability that links traditional ASW missions with missile defense.

Priority Recommendations

The CSIS study team identified seven recommendations that stand above the rest in priority. For the Baltic Sea region, there is an immediate need to deepen regional trust and facilitate information sharing among all regional partners. For the Norwegian Sea, there is an immediate need to close a key capability gap: the acoustic detection of a new generation of ultra-quiet Russian submarines.

- **Create a Baltic Sea MDA analytic center at the Baltic Maritime Component Command at Rostock.** The BMCC should immediately stand up an analytic center focused on collecting, fusing, analyzing, and then disseminating Baltic Sea MDA information. This must include information collected against relevant targets in the land domain given the nature of this littoral sea. The BMCC MDA cell should build on existing data-sharing arrangements like SUCBAS and encourage the development of the SUCBAS Level III capability to achieve sensitive data sharing. The sharing of sensitive data is necessary to drive meaningful analytic insights. The BMCC MDA fusion cell should focus on producing a common operating picture (COP) for the militaries of the region along with tailored analysis of potential threat vectors.

- o **Empower a small analytic team at the BMCC to focus on maritime hybrid issues.** A small team within the BMCC MDA fusion cell should collaborate with various governmental and nongovernmental research groups to monitor and understand maritime hybrid tactics. Consistent monitoring and assessment is vital in the Baltic Sea region due to the considerable civil maritime activity, significant seabed infrastructure, and potential novel Russian approaches. The long-term focus of this group will help senior leaders understand the susceptibility of the region to these tactics.

- o **Develop a training course for military intelligence officers on best practices for Baltic Sea MDA analysis.** The personnel component of an MDA analytic capability is often overlooked. While technology can be a crucial enabler, it cannot substitute for the value created by trained analysts knowledgeable of a given region's unique attributes and threats. Many of the Baltic Sea states do not have the capacity to sustain a training center for the discipline of a dedicated cadre of intelligence analysts. This multinational course, paired with the analytic center at Rostock, could provide a step-change improvement in the region's analytic capabilities.

- **Create a classified Baltic Sea data environment that can incorporate both NATO and partner states.** A regional MDA capability cannot be realized without a classified data environment that enables the rapid dissemination of both raw and analyzed sensor data. An integrated approach is vital. Given the importance of Finland and Sweden to the security of the Baltic Sea Region, political and military leaders in the region must summon the will to deepen real defense cooperation among the Baltic Sea nations. Building on SUCBAS Level III for data sharing may be the best way to achieve this goal, as SUCBAS already includes all the region's nations.

- **Develop a multinational operational framework for the Baltic Sea.** An integrated analytic capability is but one component of an integrated approach to the maritime issues facing the Baltic Sea. Current information-sharing agreements such as SUCFIS and SUCBAS also come up short. Political leadership throughout the region must have difficult questions about unified responses to potential Russian aggression. The response timelines in a crisis are too short for these issues to remain unanswered questions. An integrated operations framework and standardized response playbook are needed. Leadership across the region will need to harness the political will required to adopt such an approach. Given Sweden and Finland's understandable apprehension and concerns about NATO membership, a NATO "adjacent" structure is likely the best course of action. Building out the German-led BMCC may be a path forward. However, achieving an operational capability built around the BMCC will require not only regional support but also considerable German political leadership and associated investments in time, personnel, and equipment.

- **Integrate subsurface sensors and antisubmarine warfare in to a comprehensive MDA framework.** The artificial lines drawn between various aspects of the MDA puzzle run counter to achieving a holistic approach. Antisubmarine warfare must be conceptualized as an important component of MDA in both steady-state and crisis scenarios. In the Baltic, Russia may continue to use the natural stealth afforded to undersea operations to conduct an array of destabilizing and provocative operations. In the Norwegian Sea, integration of ASW into a broader domain awareness framework is key to properly cue air and missile defense assets. Understanding the undersea arena must be embraced to realize the fullness of MDA.

- **Acquire significant stockpiles of advanced sonobuoys and associated acoustic-processing systems.** The challenge of exceptionally quiet submarines requires renewed investments in deployable active and passive acoustic sensors, next-generation acoustic processing systems, and nonacoustic detection methods. In the short to mid-term, multi-static sonar arrays are the best solution and have value for both littoral ASW and open-ocean search. These next-generation sonobuoys will have to be produced and stockpiled in sufficient numbers to support both consistent use in steady-state operations and potential crisis requirements. Investments in advanced acoustic processing coupled with advanced sonobuoys can help buy back some of the lost capability in this domain. In the long term, fundamental breakthroughs in nonacoustic detection will reshape undersea warfare's hider-finder paradigm.

Other Recommendations

Beyond the above priority recommendations, there are many areas where investments are required to fully realize this vision, close identified gaps, and ensure robust capabilities for collection, analysis, and action.

Collection

- **Create resilient commercial systems.** The increased prevalence of electronic and cyber warfare operations creates challenges for air and sea traffic that rely on radar, GPS, VHF radio, and UHF radio systems. This is especially problematic in the congested Baltic Sea region. A series of mutually reinforcing systems maintains the safety of air and sea traffic. However, civil radar systems and GPS are especially susceptible to jamming. While it is ultimately up to the human operators of aircraft and ships to maintain due regard to safe operations, technical aids make the modern system of maritime and air transport possible. As it is impossible to fully harden commercial systems, civil aviation and maritime industries must ensure appropriate procedures for operations in degraded electromagnetic environments. For aviation, this effort should be led by the International Civil Aviation Organization (ICAO). For the maritime sector, this effort should be led by the International Maritime Organization (IMO). Civil operators must be prepared to identify degraded zones and reroute around these areas. At the same time, military operators must take considerable care operating powerful nonkinetic capabilities in proximity to civilian air and sea ports.

- **Ensure civil-military collaboration.** One of the largest impediments to achieving effective MDA in both basins is gaps between military and civilian agencies. In several European nations valuable MDA capabilities, such as maritime patrol aircraft, may reside solely within a civilian organization. The immediate availability and usability of these platforms during crises is unclear. Northern European nations need to ensure a standardization of tactics, techniques, and procedures for MDA activities between civil and military authorities. This standardization must include planning for the evolution of all relevant MDA capabilities to military operational control during a crisis.

- **Develop capabilities for small-signature detection.** Russia's combat swimmers, amphibious special operations forces, and other deniable military capabilities could provide it an asymmetric advantage for reconnaissance and strike missions. NATO and its partners must create a requirement for the detection, classification, and potentially prosecution of small maritime targets operating above and below the surface. This is a particularly challenging task given the small signature of these forces and the considerable background clutter in congested seas. A capability for small-signature detection must combine emerging technologies with existing acoustic detection techniques and persistent monitoring of larger host vessels to have the greatest chance for success in detecting these challenging targets.

- **Acquire a range of aerial, surface, and subsurface unmanned vehicles.** Many European militaries face tight budgets and constrained personnel. Low-cost, relatively autonomous unmanned systems, supported by automated intelligence-processing capabilities, can help reduce personnel costs and enable smaller militaries to contribute considerable capabilities. There are five classes of systems that should be procured: large unmanned aircraft (UAS), tactical UAS, counter-mine unmanned surface vessels (USVs), surveillance and intelligence USVs, sub-deployable unmanned underwater vehicles (UUVs), and air deployable UUVs.

  o *Large UAS* have payloads and flight times comparable to large manned aircraft. They have traditionally excelled in surveillance and reconnaissance roles due to their high operational altitudes and long endurance. For MDA missions, large UAS can provide persistent multimode radar coverage, carry advanced imaging sensors, conduct ELINT operations, serve as nodes for tactical networks, or carry disposable ASW payloads.

  o *Tactical UAS* have modest payloads and are primarily for visual reconnaissance or electronic collection. They can be carried by small surface vessels due to their relatively small wingspan (approximately 15 feet) and rail-launching system. When deployed in this manner, tactical UAS augment the search capabilities of manned vessels. In addition, their low cost and relative ease of operation make them valuable to small nations with limited financial and personnel resources. For MDA missions, these aircraft can provide targeted reconnaissance and surveillance capabilities.

  o *Counter-mine USVs* are small boats that clear minefields by mimicking the signatures of larger vessels to intentionally detonate mines. This brute force approach to minesweeping can be countered by advanced mines. For these threats, mine-hunting submersibles, usually tethered and remotely operated, find and disarm mines. Minesweeping USVs combined with autonomous mine hunting UUVs can help mitigate a range of mine warfare threats.

  o *ISR USVs* come in two primary varieties: positively buoyant and neutrally buoyant. The former are conventional boats that can carry a range of radar, imaging, and sonar sensors and provide formidable endurance. The latter are crosses between a surfboard and a submarine with very little visible above the waves. While these vessels can primarily carry acoustic sensors, their biggest value is their potential to serve as a persistent communications node that may be able to link submarines and UUVs into MDA networks.

- *Sub-deployable UUVs* can be used for a range of missions from surveillance of adversary port facilities to seabed warfare. These craft should be sized to fit in existing 533 mm torpedo tubes. Advances in autonomy may allow these UUVs to serve as forward warning stations for manned vessels. In this role, they would operate near adversary port facilities and transmit after detecting a vessel of interest leaving port. This cueing capability will be vital in tracking the operational patterns of advanced AIP and nuclear submarines.

- *Air-deployable UUVs* are a new type of disposable platform. These UUVs are "souped-up" sonobuoys that combine advanced acoustic sensors with some degree of locomotion. They are designed to operate for up to a week and would be used for open-ocean ASW operations in known patrol areas. Fully realizing the potential of these UUVs will require a persistent aerial communication gateway suggesting a synergy with large UAS.

- **Acquire sufficient mobile air surveillance radar capabilities to maintain persistent coverage of Baltic Sea and North Sea airspace.** As discussed in Chapter 3, there are considerable extant air surveillance capabilities across the region. However, these systems are almost all fixed and are highly vulnerable to new Russian precision-strike capabilities. For this reason, nations must acquire mobile systems that can be activated during precrisis periods to provide resilient air surveillance capabilities. With a notional range of 300 kilometers, it should be possible to adequately cover the region with the following series of mobile systems: one to two radars in Sweden, one to two radars in Finland, one radar in Latvia, one radar in Poland, two radars in Denmark, one radar in Germany, and three radars in Norway. The United Kingdom should also consider acquiring two to three mobile systems to monitor its northern periphery.

- **Acquire sufficient maritime patrol aircraft to field six 24-hour combat air patrols (CAPs) over the Baltic Sea.** Maritime patrol aircraft equipped with next-generation surveillance radars, camera systems, and air-deployable ASW sensors will be required to monitor noncompliant surface traffic and subsurface activity in this region. The radar systems on these aircraft should be multimode, capable of maritime, ground, and air moving target indicator modes to support the widest possible range of MDA activities. These aircraft should be capable of processing sensor inputs from nearby unmanned aircraft. In a degraded communications environment, onboard analytic capabilities can help mitigate bandwidth requirements. Six CAPs would provide continual coverage over the entire Baltic Sea.

This Baltic MPA capability could be shared among Germany, Poland, Denmark, and Sweden and should be integrated with increased use of unmanned platforms as described above. This capacity would only be needed during periods of increased tensions and could be regularly operated at a reduced manning level and operational tempo. This flexibility can help improve the affordability of this architecture. The multimode nature of the radar system carried on this aircraft would provide an aerial sensor layer to a regional missile defense architecture. The dual nature of these assets would enhance their cost effectiveness and suitability across the whole range of military operations.

A portion of this MPA capability may be achieved with the large UAS described above. However, considerable study will be required to validate a teamed manned-unmanned approach for the Baltic Sea region. The greatest area of concern with this approach is ensuring that the control and sensor datalinks can function in the face of advanced Russian EW and cyber capabilities. Furthermore, airspace over the Baltic Sea region may present challenges for the safe operation of unmanned aircraft in close to civil aircraft.

- **Acquire a pooled NATO MPA capability to achieve five 24-hour combat air patrols over the Norwegian Sea.** When the United Kingdom and Norway complete their procurement of P-8 Poseidon maritime patrol aircraft in 2023, there will be 14 aircraft based around this region. To further enhance regional capabilities, the Netherlands should reestablish its maritime patrol capability at a similar level to Norway. The United States should improve access and infrastructure at Keflavik, Iceland, to surge sufficient maritime patrol aircraft to contribute three to five additional CAPs as required. The United States should continue ongoing deployments to Keflavik to familiarize U.S. crews with the operating environment and manage operational tempo for allied states. The United States should also consider rotational deployments through RAF Lossiemouth in the United Kingdom and Andøya Air Station in Norway. Such rotational activities would help promote operational synergies and are similar to U.S./UK combined activities with the Rivet Joint signals intelligence aircraft.

A portion of this MPA capability may be achieved with large UAS. The issues facing UAS use in the Baltic Sea region are less acute in this basin. The threat from Russian EW is greatly reduced due to the region's geography and Norwegian Sea airspace, particularly in the northern reaches, is lightly traveled by commercial aircraft.

- **Utilize emerging space surveillance capabilities with high revisit rates to monitor ship movements.** Several commercial imaging services claim to offer daily revisit rates with relatively good resolution. For example, Planet offers "sub-weekly" revisit rates with 0.8-meter resolution.[161] BlackSky aims to launch a constellation of satellites with hourly revisit rates and 1-meter resolution.[162] These providers are using small satellites and declining launch costs to offer these capabilities at reasonable rates. While satellite imagery cannot provide persistent ship tracking, it can be a valuable tool in understanding the maritime domain, especially for noncompliant vessels. An automated analytic tool that overlays high-revisit satellite images with AIS data could locate noncooperative vessels and cue MDA assets with higher fidelity. This capability could be incredibly cost effective, optimizing the use of other MDA platforms and potentially reducing the strain on human intelligence analysts.

---

[161] Planet, "Using Space to Help Life on Earth," https://www.planet.com/company/.
[162] BlackSky, "Transforming How We Look at the Planet," https://www.blacksky.com/.

Analysis

- **Create a Norwegian Sea MDA analytic center at the newly established North Atlantic Command.** This center would mirror the body created for the Baltic Sea. It will be easier to establish and operationalize its Baltic compatriot as it will exist as a NATO body. Given the close coordination with nuclear attack submarines required for many missions in this domain, this group should be led by a U.S. Navy submariner with a British or Norwegian MPA pilot as a deputy. This MDA center should focus on understanding Russian naval activities in the North Atlantic. As a stopgap measure, the United States, United Kingdom, Norway, and the Netherlands should deepen cooperation on ASW, surface surveillance, air surveillance, and air defense missions in the North and Norwegian Seas. Given the sensitivity with which the United States and United Kingdom treat the deployment of their attack submarines, a tiered data structure may be required to push fused MDA information across the alliance.

  - **Develop a training course for military intelligence officers on best practices for Norwegian Sea MDA analysis.** This course would be like the one created for the Baltic Sea region. However, it would be tailored to the environment and threats in the Norwegian Sea. This course would prove vital in reversing the rapid decline of analytic best practices and processes. It would also help NATO establish a theater MDA capability to support steady-state and warfighting requirements.

- **Work toward increasing onboard processing capability to mitigate datalink issues.** An important element of creating a resilient MDA network is increasing onboard analytic capabilities for unmanned platforms and remote sensors. They produce huge data streams that necessitate broadband datalinks for transmission to analytic centers. This paradigm is not feasible for operations in contested electromagnetic environments and is likely not feasible for operations in noncontested environments as sensors proliferate and improve. The bandwidth will simply not exist. For this reason, sensors mounted on unmanned aircraft must have considerable capability for onboard processing and analysis so that aircraft only transmit vital information. The raw sensor data could be preserved on the aircraft for later analysis upon return to base. This technology may also help reduce the workload of sensor operators on manned MPA.

Action

- **Develop user-defined common operating pictures (COPs) to mitigate clearance issues.** This system would support a phased approach to achieving greater trust between members of an MDA network outside of an existing military alliance. The development of a user-defined COP will be vital to move fused MDA information to the myriad civil authorities in the Baltic Sea region. This information will be vital for commercial operators especially if noncooperative vessel tracks can be included without prejudicing the collection method.

- **Improve cyber resiliency of commercial systems, especially commercial port infrastructure.** The commercial maritime industry depends upon information technology to manage operations aboard ship and at sea. This infrastructure is generally poorly defended against cyber intrusions from both state and nonstate actors. The severity of this threat cannot be overstated, given the vital nature of the maritime domain to the global economy. The commercial maritime industry needs to work closely with government and other industries to adopt best practices for cybersecurity. These industries should include the banking, logistics, and utilities sectors that confront a range of threats on a daily basis. Port facilities must be treated as critical infrastructure.

- **Improve wireless datalink resiliency.** A major challenge to achieving a networked MDA capability is the susceptibility of high-bandwidth datalinks to jamming, a considerable concern in compressed geographic regions such as the Baltic Sea. Russia possesses strategic jamming systems with claimed ranges in excess of 200 km that further this threat. A growth in onboard processing capability can help to mitigate this problem. However, it cannot be solved solely through that approach. New waveforms are necessary to meet network data rate requirements while remaining resistant to nonkinetic threats. Furthermore, these wireless networks will have to have cyber resiliency baked in. The widespread, nodal nature of an MDA network creates a large surface area for a hostile agent to attack in order to reach the underlying network. The waveforms and protocols for an MDA network must be incredibly robust to ensure their resiliency in a range of scenarios, from emerging crisis through to high-end warfighting.

- **Create an MDA mesh network for the Baltic Sea.** The near certainty of the Baltic Sea region becoming a degraded EW environment during a potential contingency scenario means that new networking paradigms are required to ensure continued viability of military networks. As part of the effort to improve datalink resiliency, NATO should work to develop a mesh networking capability that can support distributed ISR and MDA sensors. Mesh networks can adapt to contested EW environments more readily than legacy systems, especially if they can integrate multiple waveforms into a cohesive network typology. This approach is likely required to respond to the highest threat environments in the Baltic Sea.

- **Rely on hardwired communications links where possible.** Advances in wireless communications over the past decades have bred a comfortable reliance by civil and military operators on these systems. For militaries operating in the Baltic Sea region, they should instead embrace hardwired datalinks wherever possible to mitigate the threat posed by jamming systems. A hardwired approach also makes considerable sense for integrating enterprise air surveillance capabilities and regional command and control networks.

Conclusion

Russia's 2014 annexation of Crimea ushered in an unfortunate new era for European defense. As NATO and its partners resolve to fill security gaps, political will and financial resources will be challenged. Not all deficiencies will be eliminated quickly, but even in a resource-constrained environment, maritime domain awareness should be a high priority. The United States and its transatlantic allies and partners must have the means to counter challenges in denied European waters. The foundation of these capabilities is an architecture for domain awareness in the European littorals and adjacent high seas. Only with reliable, actionable MDA can NATO and its partners sense and distinguish threats and respond with effect. Absent such capability, Russian activity—from criminal to coercive to combative—will be difficult to deter or defeat.

About the Authors

Andrew Metrick was an associate fellow with the International Security Program at CSIS. His work focused on relative U.S., Chinese, and Russian military capabilities, as well as maritime, unmanned, and long-range strike systems. Prior to joining CSIS, he was the team lead for the 2012–2013 "Global Go To Think Tank Index Report," responsible for a global survey process and the production of the final report. He is currently a master's candidate in the Security Studies Program at Georgetown University. He holds a B.A. in international affairs from the George Washington University with concentrations in conflict and security and international politics.

Kathleen H. Hicks is senior vice president, Henry A. Kissinger Chair, and director of the International Security Program at CSIS. With over 50 resident staff and an extensive network of nonresident affiliates, the CSIS International Security Program undertakes one of the most ambitious research and policy agendas in the security field. Dr. Hicks is a frequent writer and lecturer on geopolitics, national security, and defense matters. She served in the Obama administration as principal deputy under secretary of defense for policy and deputy under secretary of defense for strategy, plans, and forces. She led the development of the 2012 Defense Strategic Guidance and the 2010 Quadrennial Defense Review. She also oversaw Department of Defense contingency and theater campaign planning. From 2006 to 2009, Dr. Hicks served as a senior fellow in the CSIS International Security Program. From 1993 to 2006, she served as a career civil servant in the Office of the Secretary of Defense, rising from presidential management intern to the Senior Executive Service.

Dr. Hicks is concurrently the Donald Marron Scholar at the Kissinger Center for Global Affairs, Johns Hopkins School of Advanced International Studies. She serves on the Boards of Advisors for the Truman Center and SoldierStrong and is a member of the Council on Foreign Relations. Dr. Hicks served on the National Commission on the Future of the Army and currently serves on the Commission on the National Defense Strategy. She holds a Ph.D. in political science from the Massachusetts Institute of Technology, an M.P.A. from the University of Maryland, and an A.B. magna cum laude and Phi Beta Kappa from Mount Holyoke College. She is the recipient of distinguished service awards from three secretaries of defense and the chairman of the Joint Chiefs of Staff and received the 2011 DOD Senior Professional Women's Association Excellence in Leadership Award.

www.ingramcontent.com/pod-product-compliance
Lightning Source LLC
Chambersburg PA
CBHW081437270326

41932CB00019B/3237